Pronunciation Activities

Vowels in Limericks from Adam to Ursula

ARLENE EGELBERG

illustrations by Tom Milutinovic

PRO LINGUA ASSOCIATES

Pro Lingua Associates, Publishers
PO Box 1348
Brattleboro, Vermont 05302 USA
Office: 802 257 7779
Orders: 800 366 4775
E-mail: orders@ ProLinguaAssociates.com
Webstore: www.ProLinguaAssociates.com
SAN: 216-0579

At Pro Lingua

our objective is to foster an approach

to learning and teaching that we call

interplay — the interaction of language

learners and teachers with their materials,

with the language and culture, and with each other

in active, creative, and productive play.

Copyright © 1999, 2010 by Arlene Egelberg
Illustrations © 1999 Tom Milutinovic/Pannan Inc.
ISBN: 13: 978-0-86647-098-8; 10: 0-86647-098-0

Edited by Raymond C. Clark.

This book was designed and set by Judy Ashkenaz of Total Concept Associates in Brattleboro, Vermont, using Times Roman text and CityScape48 and Berthold Akzidenz Grotesk display types. Photos from Dreamstime.com Agency: Cargo, Romanian rock band © Bogdan Ionescue; Gorilla through a Knot Hole © Anthony Berenyi The book was printed and bound by Walch Publisher in Portland, Maine.

Printed in the United States of America.
Second printing 2010. 3,300 copies in print.

Contents

"Let verse run smoothly, polished with fine pumice."
                                                    —Propertius

Introduction

Pronunciation Activities: Vowels in Limericks from Adam to Ursula is especially suitable for advanced beginners and low intermediate level students, although students at higher proficiency levels will also find it very useful for polishing their pronunciation.

There are sixteen units in the text, and each unit features a limerick — a short poem. The limerick, in turn, focuses on the sound and spellings of one of the 16 vowel sounds of English. The limerick also offers excellent practice with stress, reduction, linking, intonation, and rhythm. The book is, moreover, an integrated skills text that offers lively and entertaining work on all skill areas (Speaking, Listening, Reading, Writing) within each unit.

The limerick is a light verse form that is appealing because of its humor, wordplay, and rhythm. We aren't sure of exactly how the limerick began. Some people think it was a form of popular song that Irish soldiers sang as they returned from France to Limerick, Ireland, in the eighteenth century.

The rhythm of limericks is very regular, and each limerick follows the same rhythmic pattern. Because of this, limericks offer a clear example of how stress works in English. Each limerick has five lines. The first, second, and fifth lines have three beats (stressed syllables) that are loud and long. The third and fourth lines have two beats. The other syllables are not stressed and are spoken quietly and quickly.

di DUM di DUM di DUM
di DUM di DUM di DUM
di DUM di DUM
di DUM di DUM
di DUM di DUM di DUM

Because of the importance of the stressed syllable (*DUM*) in English verse and speech, each line of the verse can have several unstressed syllables (*di*):

didi DUM didi DUM didi DUM

In short, the limerick is an excellent device for working on both the individual sounds of English (*segmentals*) and the rhythm, phrasing, and melody (*suprasegmentals*) of ordinary speech. And limericks are fun.

The appendixes contain a brief technical description of the basic features of English pronunciation, some suggestions on how to use the book, and answers to some of the exercises.

A cassette tape recording to accompany this book is available. Each of the 16 units includes the **Limerick**, the **Story**, and the **Letters** to the main character of the limerick. You may wish to listen to the cassette before you work on these three sections of the unit, or you may choose to listen after you have worked on the unit, or you can listen both before and after.

Teachers: It would be a good idea to play the cassette for yourself before you teach the unit to be sure that your pronunciation is close to the model on the cassette. Keep in mind that there are distinct differences throughout North America, and your pronunciation may differ slightly from that on the tape. The speakers on the tape are from the northern part of the United States.

If you are a non-native speaker of English, you may want to preview the recorded model before teaching the unit in your class. As suggested above, you can use the cassette in a variety of ways. The best way to use the cassette will depend on you, your students, and the context in which you are teaching.

Please note that the book can be used either with or without the cassette.

Table of Characters

1 Adam

5 Billy

2 Edna and Edward

6 Gus

3 Amy

7 Oscar

4 Rita

8 Paul

9 Joe

10 Roy

11 Brooke

12 Louis

13 Ulysses

14 Ms. Brown

15 Ivy

16 Ursula and Ernie

Table of Characters

Unit Outline

A typical unit consists of:

THE LIMERICK ILLUSTRATED: Each unit begins with an illustration of the limerick and the limerick itself. Read and begin saying the limerick and listen for the vowel focus.

SPELLING: Learn the spelling patterns of the vowel sound. Listen to and say words of one to four syllables containing the sound.

COMPARE SOUNDS AND WORDS: Practice with other sounds that are similar to the focus sound.

VOWEL HUNT: See who can find all the vowel sounds in selected newspaper ads.

COMBINE WORDS TO FORM SENTENCES: Read and say several words that contain the vowel sound, and then join the words to form sentences.

VOCABULARY: Study the definitions of some words that you will see in the story that follows, and then make complete sentences using these words.

READ: Read a short story about the limerick. Look for words that use the focus vowel sound.

SPEAK: Answer questions about the reading.

LISTEN AND SAY: Listen to the music of the limerick. Repeat it line by line. Practice saying it with special attention to the stressed syllables and words. Memorize the limerick.

EXPAND: Further explore the focus vowel or a word or expression in the limerick.

READ AND WRITE: Read short letters to limerick characters. Then write a letter to the character.

HOMONYMS: Enjoy the humor in sound-alike words. Try to guess the answer, and then check the answers in the back of the book.

Special Note

The English spelling of words is often different from their pronunciation. This is especially true with vowels. There are **five vowel letters** in English, but **sixteen vowel sounds.** The five vowel letters are:

A, a   E, e   I, i   O, o   U, u

Special phonemic symbols show the pronunciation of the different vowel sounds. In this book, the vowel sounds are shown and pronounced as follows:

SYMBOL	PRONUNCIATION	SYMBOL	PRONUNCIATION
/i/	bit, in	/u/	book, wolf
/iy/	bee, eat	/uw/	boot, true
/e/	bed, egg	/yuw/	beauty, use
/ey/	bait, age	/ow/	boat, owe
/æ/	bad, at	/ɔ/	ball, awful
/ə/	bud, under*	/oy/	boy, oil
/a/	pot, on	/ər/	bird, early
/ay/	buy, I		
/aw/	how, out		

Every word in English has at least one syllable, and each syllable contains one vowel sound. Therefore, the vowel sound is the basic unit of English pronunciation. Syllables can begin or end with one or more consonant sounds, as in the examples above: bee, eat, bed, true, wolf.

---

*The sound /ə/ is often represented with the symbol /ʌ/ when the sound is in a stressed syllable. In this book, we will use /ə/ for both the stressed and unstressed varieties.

Acknowledgments and Sources

Like folk stories and tales, limericks have come down through the years from a variety of sources. In many cases, the source is anonymous. In this collection, the following are anonymous:

"There was a young lady from Crete" (Unit 4)
"A glutton who came from the Rhine" (Unit 6)
"There was a young fellow named Paul" (Unit 8)
"There was a young girl from Asturias" (Unit 11)
"Louis made quite a to-do" (Unit 12)
"A gal who weighed many an ounce" (Unit 14)
"There was a young lady from Niger" (Unit 15)
"She frowned and said, "Now, Mr.!" (Unit 16)

I have made a few changes in some of the limericks above to suit the nature of this book. In Unit 8, the original name is "Hall." In Unit 12, "Louis" is "A diner" in the original.

Three of the limericks are attributed to individuals. I have attempted to locate these people, but even with the assistance of the Library of Congress, I have not found them. If they are still making limericks, I hope they will not mind my use of their creations.

"A canner exceedingly canny" (Unit 1) is by Carolyn Wells
"Joe'd rather have fingers than toes" (Unit 9) is by Gelett Burgess.
"There was a young fellow from Boise" (Unit 10) is by John Straley.

I have taken the liberty of changing Gelett Burgess's original, which reads, "I'd rather have fingers than toes." I hope you don't mind, Gelett, wherever you are.

And five of the limericks are my own creations:

"Edna and Edward, the elves" (Unit 2)
"Amy the Grape was her name" (Unit 3)
"A carrier pigeon named Billy" (Unit 5)
"An ostrich named Oscar would try" (Unit 7)
"Ulysses, a mule from Cathay" (Unit 13)

To my parents,
Nadya and Irving Feldman

UNIT 1
Adam

Vowel Focus: /æ/ as in <u>A</u>dam

A canner exceedingly canny,
One morning remarked to his granny,
"A canner can can
Anything that he can
But a canner can't can a can, can he?"

1.2 Spelling

The sound /æ/ is almost always written with the letter *a*. Its most common spelling pattern is *a* plus a consonant.

Examples (listen or read and say):

One syllable: **can** **had** **chat**
Two syllables: **gran** ny **ban** jo **ap** ple **car** rot
Three syllables: Su **san** nah **ap** ri cot
Four syllables: A la **ba** ma a **spa** ra gus

Add some words of your own in the spaces below:

1 Syllable	*2 Syllables*	*3 Syllables*	*4 Syllables*
_____	_____	_____	_____
_____	_____	_____	_____
_____	_____	_____	_____
_____	_____	_____	_____
_____	_____	_____	_____
_____	_____	_____	_____
_____	_____	_____	_____
_____	_____	_____	_____
_____	_____	_____	_____
_____	_____	_____	_____
_____	_____	_____	_____

Note: Some unusual spellings are: *au* as in *laugh, ai* as in *plaid*.

1.3 Compare Sounds and Words

Listen to and practice saying the three sounds below:

/æ/*	/a/	/ə/
cat	cot	cut
gnat	not	nut
hat	hot	hut
lack	lock	luck
pat	pot	putt
ran	Ron	run
rat	rot	rut

Now put the words below into the proper boxes:

mad   log   slap   battle John   socks top
shuck bottle spatter lag   stock but   stack
Jan   knack slop   sandy   block sax   tap
lug   stuck shack   bat   mud   sputter Sunday
sucks spotter shock black   knock

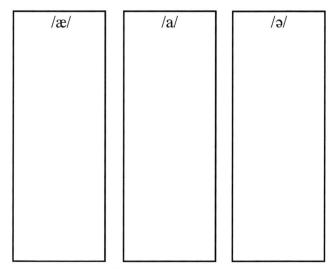

/æ/	/a/	/ə/

Answers are in the back of the book.

*These sounds are often represented with the symbol /ʌ/ when they are stressed.

1.4 Vowel Hunt

Which words in these ads use the /æ/

Antiques Show
JANUARY
1 & 2
Sat. noon–7 pm & Sun. 11 am–6 pm

Check your answers with the answers in the back of the book.

1.5 Combine Words to Form Sentences

Read the words in the lists below:

canner	Alabama	banjo	Adam
actor	Montana	piano	Amanda
landlord	Atlanta	clarinet	Janet
actress	Canada	tambourine	Samuel
dancer	Louisiana	castanets	Max

Now combine words from these lists to form sentences.

Example: An actor from Canada played the banjo for Max.

1. _____

2. _____

3. _____

4. _____

5. _____

6. _____

7. _____

8. _____

9. _____

10. _____

1.6 Vocabulary

Study the meanings of the following words:

preservation: an action that keeps something safe from harm
canner: a person who puts things in containers to keep them fresh
canny: careful, skilled, clever
exceedingly: very, extremely
remarked: said, commented
granny: informal word for grandmother
chat: talk in a friendly, informal manner

Complete these sentences with the words above:

1. The _____ is an _____ _____ person.

2. ————————— keeps things fresh.

3. Adam likes to ————————— with his friends.

4. Adam————————— to his ————————— [that] …

Answers are in the back of the book.

Look for these words in the story on the next page.

And look in a dictionary for the meaning of these related words:

uncanny: ———————————————————————

remarkable: ———————————————————————

reservation: ———————————————————————

1.7 Read

Adam

Adam puts apples, apricots, carrots, asparagus, and salmon into containers for preservation. He's a canner, of course. One Saturday in January, as Adam is chatting with his grandmother, he has a funny idea. He asks her if she thinks he can put one can into another. In other words, is it possible for him to can a can? His granny laughs.

Find 17 <u>different</u> words with the /æ/ sound in the story.

Check your answers with the answers in the back of the book.

1.8 Speak

Ask and answer these questions with a partner:

1. What's Adam's occupation?
2. How many things does he can?
3. When does he chat with his grandmother?
4. What does he ask her?
5. How would you answer Adam's question?

Talk about things you can and can't do.

1.9 Listen and Say

A **<u>can</u>ner** ex**<u>ceed</u>ingly** **<u>can</u>ny**

One **<u>morn</u>ing** re**<u>marked</u>** to his **<u>gran</u>ny,**

A **<u>can</u>ner** can **<u>can</u>**

Any<u>thing</u> that he **<u>can</u>**

But a **<u>can</u>ner** can't **<u>can</u>** a can, **<u>can</u>** he?

Practice repeating the limerick line by line. Notice the stress on the underlined syllables of the content words. Tell how many syllables each content word has, and write the number of the stressed syllable.

Word	How Many Syllables?	Which Syllable Is Stressed?
canner	2	1st
exceedingly		
canny		
morning		
remarked		
granny		
anything		

Memorize the limerick.

1.10 Expansion

The limerick is humorous because of its wordplay.

   A. *Can* can be a noun — a metal container for food, etc.
   B. *Can* can be a verb — to save by sealing in a can.
   C. *Can* can be a modal auxiliary verb — to be able to.

Tell how can is used in the sentences below (noun, verb, modal auxiliary verb).

   1. Granny cans lots of apples. _____

   2. Granny gave us a can of apples. _____

   3. Granny can make excellent apple pie. _____

When *can* is used as an auxiliary verb, it is unstressed; it sounds like "kin." Each sentence below uses *can* as an auxiliary verb. It is followed by a main verb, which is stressed.

Read and say the sentences below:

   A **dan**cer can **dan**ce.
   An **act**or can **act**.
   A **plan**ner can **plan**.
   A **nav**igator can **nav**igate.
   A **bat**ter can **bat**.

In the negative contracted form, both *can't* and the main verb are stressed. The negative uncontracted form is spelled *cannot*. *Not* is stressed.

Answer these questions. Write cannot; say can't.

Example: Who can act? (batter) The batter <u>cannot</u> act.

Who can act? (planner) _____

Who can dance? (navigator) _____

Who can navigate? (dancer) _____

Who can bat? (actor) _____

Who can plan? (batter) _____

Here are two informal meanings of *can:*

1. To tell someone they have lost their job; to dismiss; to fire.
   The boss <u>canned</u> the lazy canner.

2. To stop saying, doing, making something.
   Come on! <u>Can</u> it. That's enough.

1.11 Read — Letters to Adam

Dear Adam,

If you want to can a can, you can. It's certainly possible. But why would you want to do it? I can't understand why a can in a can is such a great idea. I say, can it!

Please write me soon, and give my regards to your granny.

Sincerely,

Patty
San Francisco

Dear Adam,

You don't know me, but I use your brand of canned food often. It's the best.

I'm curious. How many preservatives and calories are in your cans? How much cholesterol, protein, and fat do your cans contain? I'd appreciate information.

Sincerely,

Sandy
Annapolis, Maryland

Dear Adam,

The wind is blowing, the weather is cold, and I'm hungry. I see many cans of soup on my shelf, but they don't satisfy me. I want HOT SOUP in a can.

If you can can <u>hot</u> soup, you'll be very successful. Let me know what you think of my idea.

Yours truly,

Lance
Labrador, Canada

1.12 Write

Write a letter of your own to Adam the canner. Share it with the class.

Dear Adam,

1.13 Homonym

What did the rich rabbit buy?

HINT: A *carat* is a unit of weight for precious stones. One carat is 200 milligrams. Check the answer in the back ofz the book.

Notes:

UNIT 2
Edna and Edward

Vowel Focus: /e/ as in <u>E</u>dna

Edna and Edward, the elves,
Climbed up to the highest of shelves.
They came upon treasure;
They said, "What a pleasure!"
And kept everything for themselves.

2.2 Spelling

The sound /e/ is usually written with the letter *e*. Its most common spelling pattern is *e* plus a consonant. It is sometimes spelled with *ea*.

Examples (listen or read and say):

One syllable: **elf** **elves** **shelf** **shelves** **head** **spell**
Two syllables: **treas** ure **pleas** ure **bet** ter **cle** ver **wea** ther
Three syllables: for **ev** er **ev** ery where ad **ven** ture
Four syllables: in **cred** i ble **des** ti na tion

Add some words of your own in the spaces below:

1 Syllable	2 Syllables	3 Syllables	4 Syllables
————	————	————	————
————	————	————	————
————	————	————	————
————	————	————	————
————	————	————	————
————	————	————	————
————	————	————	————
————	————	————	————
————	————	————	————
————	————	————	————
————	————	————	————

Note: Some unusual spellings are: *a* in *many,* *ie* in *friend,* *ai* in *said* and *again,* *ue* in *guess.*

2.3 Compare Sounds and Words

Listen to and practice saying the two sounds below:

/æ/	/e/
mat	met
pan	pen
tan	ten
than	then
man	men
sand	send
shall	shell
sad	said
laughed	left
had	head
Annie	any

What's the word?

1. something to use in exercise class _____

2. opposite of *right* _____

3. a tool for writing _____

4. the opposite of *happy* _____

5. the past tense of *say* _____

6. a part of the body _____

7. a woman's name _____

8. something you find at the beach _____

9. something else you find at the beach _____

10. a number _____

11. the opposite of *cried* _____

12. the past tense of *meet* _____

2.4 Vowel Hunt

Identify the vowel sound /e/ in these newspaper ads:

LEXUS

The Relentless Pursuit Of Perfection.

HAVE FUN, FEEL GOOD, MAKE NEW FRIENDS

FRED ASTAIRE

FRANCHISED
DANCE STUDIOS
WINTER SPECIAL • 3 LESSONS FOR **$15**
(Limited Time Only)

GUESS
HOME COLLECTION

Check your answers with the answers in the back of the book.

2.5 Combine Words to Form Sentences

Read the words in the lists below:

Ellen	a special friend	Delaware
Emma	a clever gentleman	Connecticut
Kenneth	a French chef	Tennessee
Chelsea	ten special friends	New Mexico
Ted	seven pleasant gentlemen	Texas
Rochelle	several French chefs	Pennsylvania

Now combine words from these lists with met to form sentences.

Example: Ellen and Kenneth met a French chef in Connecticut.

1. _____
2. _____
3. _____
4. _____
5. _____
6. _____
7. _____
8. _____
9. _____
10. _____
11. _____
12. _____

2.6 Vocabulary

Study the meanings of the following words:

merry: cheerful, happy
objects: things
incredible: wonderful, unbelievable
selfish: thinking only of oneself; not thinking of others
elf, elves: a magical, imaginary fairy with pointed ears
shelf, shelves: a flat piece (often wood) fixed to a wall to hold objects
treasure: valuable things
pleasure: delight, enjoyment, feeling good
memorable: worth remembering, very interesting

Complete the sentences using these words:

One _____ Wednesday, Edna and Edward found

_____ on the highest _____ . The

_____ felt _____ because the objects

gave them a lot of _____ . The _____

elves didn't want to share their _____ with

anyone else.

Answers are in the back of the book.

Look for these words in the story on the next page.

2.7 Read

Edna and Edward

Edna and Edward were merry, clever elves who liked adventure. One memorable Wednesday, they entered a room with many shelves. When they climbed to the highest shelf, the elves were filled with pleasure. The objects on the shelf were incredible. Edna and Edward had found a treasure. Guess what? They kept everything for themselves.

Find 20 <u>different</u> words with the /e/ sound in the story. List them below:

Check your answers with the answers in the back of the book.

2.8 Speak

Ask and answer these questions with a partner:

1. Who were Edna and Edward? Describe them.
2. Why did they climb to the highest shelf?
3. How did they feel when they reached their destination?
4. What did they find?
5. What kind of treasure would *you* like to find?

2.9 Listen and Say

Edna and **Edward**, the <u>elves</u>,

Climbed <u>up</u> to the <u>highest</u> of <u>shelves</u>.

They <u>came</u> upon <u>treasure</u>;

They <u>said</u>, "What a <u>pleasure!</u>"

And <u>kept</u> every<u>thing</u> for them<u>selves</u>.

Practice repeating the limerick line by line. Notice the stress on the underlined syllables of the content words. Tell how many syllables each content word has, and write the number of the stressed syllable.

Word	*How Many Syllables?*	*Which Syllable Is Stressed?*
Edna	_____	_____
Edward	_____	_____
elves	_____	_____
shelves	_____	_____
treasure	_____	_____
pleasure	_____	_____
everything	_____	_____

Memorize the limerick.

2.10 Expansion

Many nouns ending in *f* or *fe* change the *f* to *v* and add *es* to form the plural. You have seen this change in *elf/elves* and *shelf/shelves*.

Write the plural forms of the following nouns:

wife	_____	life	_____
leaf	_____	calf	_____
thief	_____	scarf	_____
knife	_____	loaf	_____

Complete the sentences below using the plural form:

1. In winter, we often wear gloves and _____ .

2. Some people say a cat has nine _____ .

3. On a farm, there are _____ and other animals.

4. In autumn, we see many _____ on the ground.

5. _____ came into their house and stole the TV.

6. He married five times, and so he had five _____ .

7. Be careful with sharp _____ .

8. Ellen bought two _____ of bread.

2.11 Read — Letters to Edna and Edward

Dear Edna and Edward,

I heard that you found a fantastic treasure. Congratulations! I'm very happy for you. I think it will give you a lot of pleasure. I also think that I can help you if you'll share it with me. I have a lot of experience in investing, which can benefit you.

I'll call on Wednesday.

Sincerely,

Henry Ready, President
Better Investment Company

Dear Edna and Edward,

I was especially interested in your story because I like adventure, too.

Do you like to travel? Why don't you join me at Club Excellence? We have many members. We have an excellent hotel in Mexico. And every year we visit exciting destinations such as Kenya and Ecuador. I'd like to tell you about our destinations.

Please call me. I expect to hear from you soon.

Best wishes,

Beth Weathers, Club Excellence

2.12 Write

Write a letter of your own to Edna and Edward. Share it with the class.

Dear Edna and Edward,

2.13 Homonym

When she said, "I love perfume," what did he do?

HINT: *Scent* is another word for *perfume*. Check the answer in the back of the book.

Notes:

UNIT 3
Amy

Vowel Focus: /ey/ as in <u>A</u>my

Amy the Grape was her name.
Her graceful round shape brought her fame.
But she bathed in the sun,
And her shape was undone;
"I'm a raisin," she cried, "What a shame!"

3.2 Spelling

The sound /ey/ is usually written with the letters *a, a…e, ai*, and *ay*, as in *April, ace, aim, day*.

Examples (listen or read and say):

One syllable: **grape   name   shape   bathed   shame   wait   play   grain   space**

Two syllables: **A** my   **rai** sin   pa **rade**   **spa** cious

Three syllables: **a** li en   hol i **day**   va **ca** tion   **dan** ger ous

Four syllables: in vi **ta** tion   con grat u **late**

Add some words of your own in the spaces below:

1 Syllable	*2 Syllables*	*3 Syllables*	*4 Syllables*
____	____	____	____
____	____	____	____
____	____	____	____
____	____	____	____
____	____	____	____
____	____	____	____
____	____	____	____
____	____	____	____
____	____	____	____
____	____	____	____

Note: Some unusual spellings are: *eigh* as in *eight*, *ea* as in *great*, *ey* as in *they* and *obey*, *ei* as in *neighbor* and *veil*, *aigh* as in *straight*.

3.3 Compare Sounds and Words

Listen to and practice saying the two sounds below:

/ey/	/e/
main	men
raid	red
pain/pane	pen
ale/ail	el
bait	bet
date	debt
bail/bale	bell

Find a mate for these words:

Example: rake   wreck

_____   red

_____   bread

mate   _____

fade   _____

_____   cent

whale   _____

_____   west

wait   _____

late

tailor   _____

Practice saying these tongue-twisters

1. He ran rapidly in the rain.
2. Is bread good for the brain?
3. Try this taste test.
4. She tells tall tales.
5. The Red Raider wrecked the railroad train.

3.4 Vowel Hunt

Which words in these ads use the /ey/ sound?

MOVING SALE*
SAVINGS UP TO 80% OFF
OUR REGULAR PRICE

THE PAPER

An everyday adventure.

Having Our Say

Before the Pointer Sisters ...
before the Gabor Sisters ...
before the Andrews Sisters,
there were the
Delany Sisters.

WHAT'S EATING
Gilbert Grape?

Check your answers with the answers in the back of the book.

3.5 Combine Words to Form Sentences

Read the words in the lists below:

Daisy	tailor(s)	Spain
Elaine	painter(s)	Haiti
Tracy	waiter(s)	Maine
Amy	baseball player(s)	Jamaica
David	mayor(s)	Transylvania
James	trader(s)	Pennsylvania
Casey	skater(s)	Asia
Jane	caterer(s)	the Mediterranean
Grace	mason(s)	the United States
Amos	mailman (men)	Malaysia
José	sailor(s)	Romania

Now combine words from these lists to form sentences.

Example: Daisy, the waiter, came to the United States from Haiti.

1. _____

2. _____

3. _____

4. _____

5. _____

6. _____

7. _____

8. _____

9. _____

10. _____

11. _____

3.6 Vocabulary

Study the meanings of the following words:

graceful: beautiful in form, manner, and movement
shape: form
sunbathe: sit or lie in strong sunlight
wrinkled: not smooth
undone: ruined, destroyed
What a shame! How sad! How unfortunate! Too bad!
famous: well known

Complete the sentences using these words:

1. Amy's _____ was _____ because she went _____ on the beach.

2. The old man's face was _____ .

3. _____ dancers are always _____ .

4. She sadly remarked, _____ .

Answers are in the back of the book.

Look for these words in the story on the next page.

3.7 Read

Amy

Amy was a tasty grape who was famous for her graceful shape. One day when Amy was on vacation, she felt lazy. Amy found a comfortable place in the sun and stayed there for eight hours. Sunbathing is not a good idea for a grape. After sunbathing for eight hours, Amy looked in the mirror. She had changed. Poor Amy was now small and wrinkled. Amy had become a raisin. Wasn't that a shame?

Find 16 <u>different</u> words with the /ey/ sound in the story. List them below:

Check your answers with the answers in the back of the book.

3.8 Speak

Ask and answer these questions with a partner:

1. Who was Amy? Describe her.
2. Why was she famous?
3. How did she feel when she was on vacation?
4. How long did Amy bathe in the sun?
5. What did she become?
6. What's your opinion about sunbathing?

3.9 Listen and Say

Amy the **Grape** was her **name**.

Her **graceful** round **shape** brought

   her **fame**.

But she **bathed** in the **sun**,

And her **shape** was **undone**.

"I'm a **raisin**," she **cried**. "What

   a **shame**!"

Practice repeating the limerick line by line. Notice the stress on the underlined syllables of the content words. Tell how many syllables each content word has, and write the number of the stressed syllable.

Word	How Many Syllables?	Which Syllable Is Stressed?
Amy	_____	_____
graceful	_____	_____
shape	_____	_____
bathed	_____	_____
undone	_____	_____
raisin	_____	_____
shame	_____	_____

Memorize the limerick.

3.10 Expansion

Undone is an adjective that has three meanings:

1. unfastened
2. not finished
3. ruined

Which meanings fit the sentences below?

1. The new building is still undone. _____

2. When she turned around, her bow came undone. _____

? 3. Amy's shape was undone. _____

Many words can be made negative by adding un. Here are a few. Add an un and use them in a sentence:

planned	successful	satisfying	believable
happy	exciting	expected	comfortable
changed	wise	necessary	attractive

_____

_____

_____

_____

_____

_____

_____

_____

_____

_____

3.11 Read — Letters to Amy

Dear Amy,

How are you doing? Many of your friends are sitting comfortably in my refrigerator.

I like sunbathing, too. However, it's unwise for people and grapes to sunbathe for a long time. Please don't cry. It isn't necessary for you to be sad. Your wrinkled face is rather attractive.

I hope that you will learn to love yourself as you are.

Sincerely,

Jason
Cape May, NJ

Dear Amy,

I hear that you're very sad to be a raisin. Maybe you should go to the beauty parlor for a body treatment. I'm sure that will make you feel better about yourself. Anyway, don't worry about it. It's not so bad. You know, raisins are very famous.

If you have any questions, you can write to me. I'll try to help you.

Sincerely,

Kate
Monterey, CA

3.12 Write

**Write a letter of your own to Amy the Grape.
Share it with the class.**

Dear Amy,

3.13 Homonym

If four couples went to a restaurant, how many people had dinner?

HINT: What's the past tense of *eat*? Check the answer in the back of the book.

Notes:

UNIT 4
Rita

Vowel Focus: /iy/ **as in Rita**

There was a young lady from Crete,
Who was so exceedingly neat,
When she got out of bed,
She stood on her head
To make sure of not soiling her feet.

4.2 Spelling

The sound /iy/ is usually written with the letters *e, ee, ea, e...e, ie,* and *y*:

e as in *be, me*   *ee* as in *three, feet*
ea as in *sea, reason*   *e...e* as in *Crete, here*
ie as in *believe, brief*   *y* as in *friendly*

Examples (listen or read and say):

One syllable: **Crete   neat   feet   meet   he   please**
Two syllables: **rea** son   **crea** ture   be **lieve**   **ei** ther
Three syllables: pro **ced** ure   **mean** ing ful   hap pi **ly**
Four syllables: ex **ceed** ing ly   In do **ne** sia

Add some words of your own in the spaces below:

1 Syllable	*2 Syllables*	*3 Syllables*	*4 Syllables*
_____	_____	_____	_____
_____	_____	_____	_____
_____	_____	_____	_____
_____	_____	_____	_____
_____	_____	_____	_____
_____	_____	_____	_____
_____	_____	_____	_____
_____	_____	_____	_____
_____	_____	_____	_____

Note: Some unusual spellings are: *ey* in *money, i...e* in *machine, ei* in *receive, i* in *taxi, eo* in *people*.

4.3 Compare Sounds and Words

Listen to and practice saying the two sounds below:

/iy/	/e/
feed	fed
meet/meat	met
neat	net
peak/peek	peck
seal	sell
teak	tech
seed	said
weed	wed
wheel	well

Read these sentences aloud:

1. She said it was a seed.
2. They met at the meeting.
3. Do they sell meat?
4. Can we feed the seal?
5. He did well at the wheel.

Write some sentences of your own. Use one /iy/ sound and one /e/ sound in each sentence.

_____

_____

_____

_____

_____

_____

_____

4.4 Vowel Hunt

Identify the vowel sound /iy/ in these newspaper ads:

CITIBANK

6218 1901 190 190

THE **CITI** NEVER SLEEPS

ANTIQUES

Beef.

Real food for real people.

Easter Bunny

Tiffany's floral rabbit in glazed earthenware.
6 1/2" high, $32. To order, please call 800-526-0649.

Check your answers with the answers in the back of the book.

4.5 Combine Words to Form Sentences

Read the words in the lists below:

Maria	meat	Sweden
Rico	beet(s)	Korea
Gene/Jean	cheese	Egypt
Amy	sardine(s)	Vienna
Edith	ice cream	Phoenix
Steve	roast beef	Greenland
Casey	peach(es)	Greece
Leo	pizza	Indonesia
Emile	turkey	Argentina
Dean	cookie(s)	Missouri

Now combine words from these lists to form sentences.

Examples: Leo never eats meat in Argentina.

Steve treated Edith to pizza in Sweden.

(One meaning of the verb *treat* is to invite someone to be your guest — to pay for another person.)

1. _____

2. _____

3. _____

4. _____

5. _____

6. _____

7. _____

8. _____

9. _____

4.6 Vocabulary

Study the meanings of the following words:

Crete: a Greek island
make sure: be certain
soil: make dirty
neat: not messy, in orderly condition
extreme(ly): very, very
seem: appear to be

Complete the sentences using these words:

1. The lady from _____ was exceedingly _____ .

   _____

2. She wanted to _____ _____ that she would

   not _____ her feet.

3. Doesn't her idea _____ strange?

4. Yes, it's an _____ weird idea.

Answers are in the back of the book.

Write some sentences of your own with these words:

_____

_____

_____

_____

_____

Look for these words in the story on the next page.

4.7 Read

Rita

Rita was a neat and clean young lady from the Greek island of Crete. In fact, she was extremely clean. In the morning, when she got out of bed, Rita was afraid that she'd get her feet dirty. Therefore, she kept them off the ground. Rita stood on her head to keep her feet clean. Doesn't that seem weird?

Find 12 <u>different</u> words with the /iy/ sound in the story. List them below:

Check your answers with the answers in the back of the book.

4.8 Speak

Ask and answer these questions with a partner:

1. Who was Rita? Describe her.
2. Where did Rita come from?
3. When did Rita feel afraid?
4. How did she keep her feet off the ground?
5. What would you do if you were Rita?
6. Are you a neat person? a messy person? What does being neat or messy mean? Discuss this with your partner.

4.9 Listen and Say

There **was** a young **lady** from **Crete,**

Who **was** so **exceedingly neat,**

When she **got** out of **bed,**

She **stood** on her **head**

To make **sure** of not **soiling** her **feet.**

Practice repeating the limerick line by line. Notice the stress on the underlined syllables of the content words. Tell how many syllables each content word has, and write the number of the stressed syllable.

Word	*How Many Syllables?*	*Which Syllable Is Stressed?*
lady	_____	_____
Crete	_____	_____
exceedingly	_____	_____
neat	_____	_____
soiling	_____	_____

Memorize the limerick.

4.10 Expansion

/iy/ is the sound we use in *the* when it is followed by a word beginning with a vowel sound. Otherwise, *the* is pronounced with the vowel /ə/ (Unit 6).

Read and say the examples below:

the astronaut	the adventure	the infant
the aim	the exhibition	the egg
the eel	the ice	the ocean
the umbrella	the hour	the elves
the actor	the apricot	the investment

Find 10 interesting nouns or adjectives that begin with vowel sounds. Write them below.

Examples: the <u>adjective</u>
  the <u>interesting</u> adjective

_____

_____

_____

_____

_____

_____

_____

_____

_____

_____

_____

4.11 Read — Letters to Rita

Dear Rita,

I think you are very busy keeping your feet clean, aren't you? How do you feel when you stand on your head? Is it comfortable?

If I were you, I would put on shoes and put a clean carpet on the floor. If your floor is clean, you don't have to worry about making your feet dirty.

Your friend,

Doreen, Murfreesboro, Tennessee

Dear Rita,

I read your story. I agree with you that it's very important to be neat and clean, but you are being extreme about this. People will think you are weird -- even crazy.

You want to keep your feet clean, but what about your head? Do you want to make your head dirty? It is the same thing. I believe you need help.

You should make an appointment with a psychiatrist. Maybe he or she can help you see that you need to change your ideas.

Sincerely,

Marie, New Orleans, Louisiana

4.12 Write

Write a letter of your own to Rita. Share it with the class.

Dear Rita,

4.13 Homonym

Why did the mountaineer need binoculars?

HINT: Another word for *look* is *peek* — to look quickly. And what is the very top of the mountain called? Check the answer in the back of the book.

Notes:

UNIT 5
Billy

Vowel Focus: /i/ as in B<u>i</u>lly

A carrier pigeon named Billy,
While delivering a message to Chile,
Falls madly in love
With a Chilean dove;
He won't up and leave her now, will he?

5.2 Spelling

The sound /i/ is usually written with the letter *i*. Its most common spelling pattern is *i* plus a consonant.

Examples (listen or read and say):

One syllable: **this   is   his   still**
Two syllables: **pi** geon   **win** dy   **chil** ly
Three syllables: ter **ri** fic   **li** mer ick
Four syllables: **Cin** cin nat i   **Mis** sis **sip** pi

Add some words of your own in the spaces below:

1 Syllable	2 Syllables	3 Syllables	4 Syllables
————	————	————	————
————	————	————	————
————	————	————	————
————	————	————	————
————	————	————	————
————	————	————	————
————	————	————	————
————	————	————	————
————	————	————	————
————	————	————	————

Note: Other spellings are: *y* as in *Olympic* and *mystery; e* as in *pretty* and *English, ee* as in *been, ui* as in *build, u* as in *busy, o* as in *women.*

5.3 Compare Sounds and Words

Listen to and practice saying the three sounds below:

/e/	/i/	/iy/
set	sit	seat
net	knit	neat
tech	tick	teak
sex	six	seeks
pet	pit	peat
met	mitt	meat
said	Sid	seed
ten	tin	teen

What's the word?

1. a kind of glove _____

2. something to eat _____

3. a number _____

4. what cans are made of _____

5. how you make a sweater _____

6. a young person _____

7. an animal _____

8. very orderly _____

9. something that grows _____

10. a hole _____

5.4 Vowel Hunt

Which words in these ads use the /i/ sound?

CLINT   MERYL
EASTWOOD   STREEP

THE **BRIDGES** OF
MADISON
COUNTY

Singapore:
An orchid in the Pacific

FINNAIR
Uncommon Concern For The Individual

Check your answers with the answers in the back of the book.

5.5 Combine Words to Form Sentences

Read the words in the lists below:

Mickey	sibling(s)	Virginia
Minnie	sister	India
Elizabeth	twins	Disneyland
William	triplets	England
Richard		
Jim		

Now combine words from these lists to form 5 sentences.

Examples: Mickey and Minnie are twins from India.
Jim and his siblings live in Virginia.

1. _____

2. _____

3. _____

4. _____

5. _____

5.6 Vocabulary

Study the meanings of the following words:

carrier pigeon: a bird that carries messages and finds its way back
  home
Chilean: from the South American country of Chile
deliver: carry, bring and leave something
smitten*: to be affected or hit in a strong way

*Some idioms that mean "very much in love" (*smitten*) are: *madly in love, head over heels in love, swept off one's feet.*

Complete the sentences using the words above:

1. Billy is a _____ _____ .

2. He travels to Chile in order to_____ a message.

3. Billy meets a pretty _____ dove and falls in love. He

   is _____ .

Answers are in the back of the book.

Write some sentences of your own with these words:

_____

_____

_____

_____

_____

_____

Look for these words in the story on the next page.

5.7 Read

Billy

A carrier pigeon named Billy lives in Finland.
His job is to bring messages to far-away places,
and then quickly fly home. One windy, wintry
day, Billy delivers a message to Chile and meets
a pretty Chilean dove. Her name is Linda, and,
in a minute, Billy is smitten. Now he has a big
problem. Billy knows he should fly home, but it
seems impossible for him to leave Linda.

Find 21 <u>different</u> words with the /i/ sound in the story. List them below:

Check your answers with the answers in the back of the book.

5.8 Speak

Ask and answer these questions with a partner:

1. Where does Billy live?
2. What is his job?
3. When does Billy deliver a message to Chile?
4. Whom does he meet?
5. Why does Billy have a problem?
6. Would you give up your job and live in a new country for love? Discuss this with your partner.

5.9 Listen and Say

A **carrier pigeon** named **Billy**

While **delivering** a **message**

  to **Chile,**

Falls **madly** in **love**

With a **Chilean dove;**

He **won't** up and **leave** her

  now, **will** he?

Practice repeating the limerick line by line. Notice the stress on the underlined syllables of the content words.

Word	How Many Syllables?	Which Syllable Is Stressed?
carrier	_____	_____
pigeon	_____	_____
Billy	_____	_____
message	_____	_____
Chile	_____	_____

The phrase "up and leave" is an idiomatic preposition and verb combination. The "up" gives the idea of "suddenly."

Memorize the limerick.

5.10 Expansion

Tag questions:

Tag questions have two parts. The first part makes a statement. The second part is a question that usually asks for agreement with or confirmation of the statement. The tag uses an auxiliary verb (*do, be, have,* and modals) and a pronoun.

> *Example:* Billy <u>won't</u> up and leave her now, <u>will he</u>?

Notice that we use an affirmative tag with a negative statement (above), and a negative tag with an affirmative statement (below).

> *Examples:* Billy stayed in Chile, <u>didn't he</u>?
> He can find a job in Chile, <u>can't he</u>?

Use the sentences you wrote in section 5.3 to form tag questions.

> *Example:* Mickey and Minnie are twins from India,
> aren't they?

_____

_____

_____

_____

_____

_____

_____

_____

_____

_____

5.11 A Crossword of Tags

Across:

3. The treasure was incredible, _____ ?

6. If Brooke threw eggs at someone, they'd probably break, _____ ?

7. The lady of Crete hoped that she would keep her feet clean, _____ ?

9. The elves will always be happy with their treasure, _____ ?

11. I'm the best cook in the world, _____ ?

14. The glutton and I really shouldn't eat so much, _____ _____ ?

15. That man isn't Billy, _____ ?

Down:

1. I can can cans better than the canner, _____ ?

2. You don't like Ms. Brown, _____ ?

4. Ms. Brown's chair should be sturdier, _____ ?

5. She's a very good granny, _____ ?

8. We haven't had a new limerick this week, _____ ?

10. I won't have to attend Paul's funeral, _____ ?

11. I'm not supposed to eat this, _____ ?

12. This book isn't difficult, _____ ?

13. I don't have to kiss Ursula, _____ ?

5.12 Read — Letters to Billy

Dear Billy,

Why don't you invite Linda to live in Finland? It's a very interesting country. She can leave Chile with you, and your big problem is solved.

Sincerely,

Ms. Phyllis Fixit
Philadelphia

Dear Billy,

I think I understand you because I had a similar experience. I used to travel in my job, too, flying all over the world. Then I met Millicent on a trip to England and didn't want to leave. I proposed marriage and quit my job. Now Millicent and I live happily together in our little nest in Liverpool.

All my best,

Winston
Liverpool, England

Dear Billy,

You'd be silly to leave Chile and Linda. Why come back to chilly Finland? And why leave a chick like Linda?

You're in love, aren't you?
Chile is beautiful, isn't it?
I'm right, aren't I?

So say you'll stay, won't you?
And I can visit, can't I?

Sincerely,

Your nest-mate, Sidney
Helsinki

5.13 Write

Write a letter of your own to Billy. Share it with the class.

Dear Billy,

5.14 Homonym

What did Jim call his exercise clubs?

HINT: What is the name of the place where people exercise?

Notes:

Review

Without looking back, review Units 1–5 by yourself, with a partner, or with a small group:

- First, tell each character's story.

- Next, try to say the limerick.

- When you have finished, look back at the five units.

- Finally, decide which limerick you like best and why. Then discuss your ideas with others.

UNIT 6
Gus

Vowel Focus: /ə/ as in G<u>u</u>s

A glutton who came from the Rhine
Was asked at what hour he'd dine.
He replied, "At eleven,
At three, five, and seven,
And eight and a quarter to nine."

6.2 Spelling

The sound /ə/ is usually written with the letters *u* or *o* when the sound is stressed.

>   ***Examples:*** S<u>u</u>nday, M<u>o</u>nday

Other spellings are: *ou* as in *double* or *enough*, *oe* as in *does*, and *oo* as in *flood*. Also note that many books write this stressed sound as /ʌ/.

However, when a vowel sound in English is not stressed, the sound often becomes the unstressed /ə/. This sound (called *schwa*) is the most common vowel sound in English. It is usually spoken with very little energy because it has very little stress, and it may be spelled with any of the vowel letters:

a	<u>a</u>bove	*e*	h<u>e</u>llo	*i*	m<u>i</u>stake
o	t<u>o</u>morrow	*u*	s<u>u</u>ppose		

Examples (listen or read and say):

The unstressed /ə/ is underlined.

One syllable: **sun** **son** **just** **tough**
Two syllables: **some** thing **glut** <u>ton</u> **doz** <u>en</u> **Lon** <u>don</u>
Three syllables: **gov** ern <u>ment</u> **won** der <u>ful</u> hol <u>i</u> day
Four/five syllables: in <u>vi</u> ta <u>tion</u> <u>pro</u> **nun** ci a <u>tion</u>

Add some words of your own in the spaces below:

1 Syllable	*2 Syllables*	*3 Syllables*	*4 Syllables*
————	————	————	————
————	————	————	————
————	————	————	————
————	————	————	————
————	————	————	————

6.3 Compare Sounds and Words

Listen to and practice saying the five sounds below:

/əe/	/e/	/i/	/a/	/ə/
gnat	net	knit	knot	nut
tack	tech	tick	tock	tuck
bag	beg	big	bog	bug

What's the word?

1. another word for *insect* _____

2. something you tie _____

3. the opposite of *little* _____

4. something to eat _____

5. one way to catch fish _____

6. a word where *ch* sounds like *k* _____

7. to make a sweater _____

8. to plead _____

9. the sounds a clock makes _____

10. a wet, muddy place _____

6.4 Vowel Hunt

Identify the vowel sound /ə/ in these newspaper ads:

SOTHEBY'S
FOUNDED 1744
1334 York Avenue at 72nd Street, New York, NY 10021 • (212) 606-7000

THE PHANTOM
OF THE OPERA
MAJESTIC THEATRE

Check your answers with the answers in the back of the book.

6.5 Combine Words to Form Sentences

Read the words in the lists below:

Douglas	a hundred	bun(s)	butter
Dudley	a dozen	cupcake(s)	honey
Justine	twenty	pumpkin pie(s)	mustard
Melinda	a couple of	muffin(s)	
Russell	one	cutlet(s)	
Sonny	some	onion(s)	
Elizabeth		mussel(s)	
		mushroom(s)	

Now combine words from these lists to form 10 sentences. Then tell who was/wasn't a glutton.

Examples: Dudley ate a hundred buns with butter. He was a glutton.
Douglas ate one bun with butter. He wasn't a glutton.

1. _____

2. _____

3. _____

4. _____

5. _____

6. _____

7. _____

8. _____

9. _____

10. _____

6.6 Vocabulary

Study the meanings of the following words:

glutton: a person who eats too much
Rhine: an area and river in Germany
reply: to answer
dine: to eat (somewhat formal)

Complete the sentences using the words above:

1. Only one person _____ to the question.

2. A person who eats too much is a _____ .

3. The _____ river is in Germany.

4. The rich and famous often _____ at Emilio's Restaurant.

5. Please _____ by August 31st.

Answers are in the back of the book.

Write some sentences of your own with these words:

_____

_____

_____

_____

_____

_____

Look for these words in the story on the next page.

6.7 Read

Gus

Gus was a man from the Rhine who weighed
three hundred twenty-one pounds. He was called
a glutton because he ate too much and too often.
One day he was asked when he wanted to dine.
Gus replied with six different times as his answer. Do you think he was really that hungry?

**Find 13 <u>different</u> words with the stressed or
unstressed /ə/ sound in the story. Which two
words have both stressed and unstressed
/ə/ in them?**

Stressed (6)   *Unstressed (7)*

Check your answers with the answers in the back of the book.

6.8 Speak

**Ask and answer these questions with a
partner:**

1. Where did Gus come from?
2. Why was he called a glutton?
3. What question was he asked?
4. How did he answer the question?
5. How would you answer the same question?

6.9 Listen and Say

A **glutton** who **came** from the **Rhine**

Was **asked** at what **hour** he'd **dine**.

He re**plied,** "At e**lev**en,

At **three,** five, and **sev**en,

And **eight** and a **quar**ter to **nine**."

Practice repeating the limerick line by line. Notice the stress on the underlined syllables of the content words. Tell how many syllables each content word has. Write the number of the stressed syllable.

Word	How Many Syllables?	Which Syllable Is Stressed?
glutton	_____	_____
replied	_____	_____
eleven	_____	_____
seven	_____	_____
quarter	_____	_____

List the words in the limerick with the unstressed /ə/ sound below:

Memorize the limerick.

6.10 Expansion

Idioms – read the definitions below:

gulp down: to swallow or drink a large amount quickly.
The glutton gulped down his dinner.
polish off: to finish completely.
He polished off two sandwiches in a minute.
half-baked: not very sensible; crazy.
Your plan is simply half-baked.
hard-boiled: tough and not very sensitive to feelings.
The hard-boiled policeman didn't even smile.
square meal: a well-balanced meal
I haven't had a square meal in days.
spill the beans: to tell a secret.
I think they know. Did somebody spill the beans?
take with a grain of salt: to not believe the entire story.
She says she has lost thirty pounds, but I'd take that with a grain of salt.

Write some sentences of your own using the idioms above:

_____

_____

_____

_____

_____

_____

_____

_____

_____

6.11 Read — Letters to Gus

Dear Gus,

I'd like to ask you an important question. If you spend so much time eating, when do you do other important things in life?

Do you have any time for reading, exercising, working, caring for your family, or making friends? Do you have any time to walk on the beach or look at the stars? There's more to life than eating.

Sincerely,

Judd
Columbus, Georgia

Dear Gus,

We have something in common. I love to eat, too, but we have different ideas about <u>when</u> to eat. I eat only two or three times a day, and I'm thin. You eat all day, and you're overweight.

Do you want to change yourhabits? Do you want to lose weight? I will help you. When do you want to meet?

Sincerely,

Justin
Edmundston, New Brunswick

Dear Gus,

I want to know why you eat so much. It is not healthy for you.

If you eat excessively, you can get sick. Also, you will be out of shape. I advise you to eat a balanced diet. Eat plenty of fruit and vegetables. Eat only three square meals a day. If you take my advice, you'll live longer.

Sincerely,

Humphrey
London

6.12 Write

Write a letter of your own to Gus. Share it with the class.

Dear Gus,

6.13 Homonym

How many people won the race?

HINT: You can't have two winners.

Notes:

Word Search

Write Find 20 words with the /ə/ sound.

A Wordsearch Puzzle for Gus

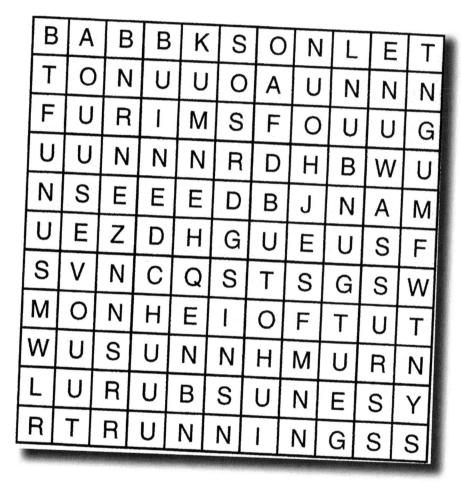

B	A	B	B	K	S	O	N	L	E	T
T	O	N	U	U	O	A	U	N	N	N
F	U	R	I	M	S	F	O	U	U	G
U	U	N	N	N	R	D	H	B	W	U
N	S	E	E	E	D	B	J	N	A	M
U	E	Z	D	H	G	U	E	U	S	F
S	V	N	C	Q	S	T	S	G	S	W
M	O	N	H	E	I	O	F	T	U	T
W	U	S	U	N	N	H	M	U	R	N
L	U	R	U	B	S	U	N	E	S	Y
R	T	R	U	N	N	I	N	G	S	S

UNIT 7
Oscar

Vowel Focus: /a/ as in Oscar

An ostrich named Oscar would try
To imitate birds in the sky,
Till one day his father
Said, "Oscar, don't bother;
It's honestly pie in the sky."

7.2 Spelling

The sound /a/ is usually written with the letter *o*. Its most common spelling pattern is *o* plus a consonant.

Examples (listen or read and say):

One syllable: **on**   **odd**   **stop**   **got**
Two syllables: **Os** car   **os** trich   **both** er   **fol** low   **sor** ry
Three syllables: **con** so nant   **hon** est ly
Four syllables: im **pos** si ble

Add some words of your own in the spaces below:

1 Syllable	*2 Syllables*	*3 Syllables*	*4 Syllables*

Note: Other spellings are: *a* as in *want*, *watch*, and *father*; *ea* as in *heart*; *ow* as in *knowledge*; *e* as in *ensemble* and *encore*.

7.3 Compare Sounds and Words

Listen to and practice saying the four sounds below:

/æ/	/e/	/i/	/a/
gnat	net	knit	knot/not
tack	tech	tick	tock
knack	neck	nick	knock
sax	sex	six	socks
pat	pet	pit	pot
rack	wreck	Rick	rock
sad	said	Sid	sod

What's the word?

1. something to cook in _____

2. part of your body _____

3. a number _____

4. a musical instrument _____

5. a small nail _____

6. touch lightly _____

7. make a noise on a door _____

8. something you wear _____

9. a stone _____

10. a destroyed car _____

7.4 Vowel Hunt

Which words in these ads use the /a/

THE DOCUMENT COMPANY
XEROX

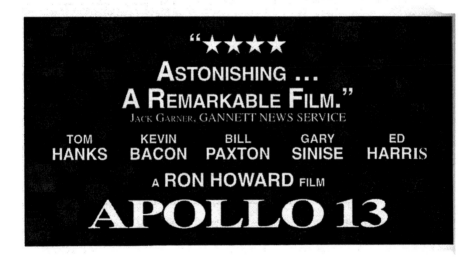

OPERATION
DUMBO DROP

"★★★★
ASTONISHING ...
A REMARKABLE FILM."
JACK GARNER, GANNETT NEWS SERVICE

TOM   KEVIN   BILL   GARY   ED
HANKS   BACON   PAXTON   SINISE   HARRIS

A RON HOWARD FILM

APOLLO 13

Check your answers with the answers in the back of the book.

7.5 Combine Words to Form Sentences

Read the words in the lists below:

Molly	golf	Oregon
Robert	volleyball	Colorado
Connie	the concertina	Florida
Thomas	Ping-Pong	Wisconsin
John	soccer	Nevada
Polly	hockey	Ontario

Now combine words from these lists and use the verb play to form 10 sentences.

Example: Molly and Robert want to play Ping-Pong
in Nevada.

_____

_____

_____

_____

_____

_____

_____

_____

_____

_____

7.6 Vocabulary

Study the meanings of the following words:

spread: to open, stretch
ostrich: the largest living bird
imitate: follow in action or manner; do the same thing
don't bother: don't do something because it is unnecessary or
    impossible
energy: power, strength
waste: to use carelessly

Complete the sentences using the words above:

1. An _____ can't fly.

2. Don't _____ your money on that.

3. Oscar tried to _____ other birds.

4. He watched them _____ their wings.

5. Oscar used a lot of _____ when he tried to fly.

6. Oscar's father said, " _____ ."

Answers are in the back of the book.

Write some sentences of your own with these words:

_____

_____

_____

_____

Look for these words in the story on the next page.

7.7 Read

Oscar

Oscar was a young ostrich who wanted to be like other birds. Oscar watched the other birds spread their wings and fly, and he wanted to fly, too. Every day he tried to imitate them, but Oscar never got off the ground. Oscar's father was sorry to see his son wasting his energy. He told Oscar to stop trying to do impossible things. He said it was "pie in the sky."

Find 10 <u>different</u> words with the /a/ sound in the story. List them below:

Check your answers with the answers in the back of the book.

7.8 Speak

Ask and answer these questions with a partner:

1. Who was Oscar? Describe him.
2. What did he try to do?
3. How did his father feel about it?
4. Why did Oscar's father discourage him?
5. What would you do if you were Oscar?

7.9 Listen and Say

An **ostrich** named **Oscar** would **try**

To **imitate** **birds** in the **sky**.

Till **one** day his **father**

Said, "**Oscar**, don't **bother**;

It's **honestly** **pie** in the **sky**."

Practice repeating the limerick line by line. Notice the stress on the underlined syllables of the content words. Tell how many syllables each content word has. Write the number of the stressed syllable.

Word	How Many Syllables?	Which Syllable Is Stressed?
ostrich	_____	_____
Oscar	_____	_____
imitate	_____	_____
father	_____	_____
bother	_____	_____
honestly	_____	_____

List the words in the limerick with the /a/ sound below:

Memorize the limerick.

7.10 Expansion

Idioms

Sometimes you can guess the meaning of idioms. Try to create definitions for these idioms and then compare your answers with others'. Finally, look them up in a dictionary or an idiom book.

> That's <u>pie in the sky</u>.
> I'm sorry, but you can't <u>have your cake and eat it, too</u>.
> It's gone. It doesn't make sense to <u>cry over spilled milk</u>.
> Come on! Enjoy yourself! Don't be a <u>wet blanket</u>!
> Give up! I think you're looking for <u>a needle in a haystack</u>.
> The police said they will <u>leave no stone unturned</u>.
> Do you believe that? I think it's a lot of <u>hot air</u>.
> That's not such a <u>big deal</u>. You're making <u>a mountain out of a mole hill</u>.

Write some sentences of your own using the idioms above:

_____

_____

_____

_____

_____

_____

_____

_____

_____

_____

7.11 Read — Letters to Oscar

Dear Oscar,

I guess you are trying to imitate birds in the sky. You know, dreamers almost all experienced failure at first. But they continued to believe in their ideas. I think you will be able to imitate birds in the future. Other people may laugh at you, but remember that almost all inventors, dreamers, and innovators were laughed at and called stupid. However, in the end, they were successful.

Sincerely,

Wanda, Walla Walla, Washington

Dear Oscar,

Why do you want to fly? If you are really serious, you should take a plane because your wings are too small. Your father said that wanting to fly was "pie in the sky." I think he was right.

Oscar, I'd like to give you some advice. According to the newspapers and magazines, this is a special discount season for air travel. It's a great opportunity to buy an inexpensive ticket. Go for it!

Sincerely,

Bob, Oshkosh, Wisconsin

7.12 Write

Write a letter of your own to Oscar. Share it with the class.

Dear Oscar,

7.13 Homonym

What did the hunter aim at?

HINT: A *hart* is a kind of deer.

Notes:

UNIT 8
Paul

Vowel Focus: /ɔ/ as in P<u>au</u>l

There was a young fellow named Paul,
Who fell in the spring in the fall.
'T would have been a sad thing
Had he died in the spring,
But he didn't — he died in the fall.

8.2 Spelling

The sound /ɔ/ is usually written with the letters *o, a, au,* and *aw:*

> *o* as in *office*
> *a* as in *call, warm*
> *au* as in *August, cause*
> *aw* as in *draw, awful*

Examples (listen or read and say):

One syllable: **paw   dog   long   mall   chalk   taught   boss**
Two syllables: a **cross**   **al** ways   **quart** er   **awe** some   **aud** it
Three syllables: **al** read y   **or** gan ize
Four syllables: **cor** por a tion   **au** to mo bile

Add some words of your own in the spaces below:

1 Syllable	2 Syllables	3 Syllables	4 Syllables
————	————	————	————
————	————	————	————
————	————	————	————
————	————	————	————
————	————	————	————
————	————	————	————
————	————	————	————
————	————	————	————
————	————	————	————

Note: Other spellings are: *augh* as in *daughter, ough* as in *bought,* and *oa* as in *broad.*

8.3 Compare Sounds and Words

Listen to and practice saying the sounds below:

/ɔ/	/ow/
Paul	pole
called	cold
bald	bold, bowled
hall	hole, whole

Practice reading and saying the following sentences aloud:

Paul climbed a pole and told the bold, bald man to hold it.
Walter called the owner about the cold and the hole in the wall.

Write some silly sentences of your own using /ɔ/ and /ow/ words. Here are a few more:

all	ball	cloth	false	fault
loss	ought	pause	raw	salt
sauce	saw	small	soft	straw

_____

_____

_____

_____

_____

_____

8.4 Vowel Hunt

Which words in these ads use the /ɔ/ sound?

To brighten your home and warm your heart ...
Norman Rockwell Lighted Christmas Village

North Shore
Animal League
Lewyt Street • Port Washington

Water
BABIES
by **Coppertone**
SPF **45**

NORDSTROM
THE MALL AT SHORT HILLS

Oral-B *Tooth and Gum Care*
Patented Stannous Fluoride Toothpaste

Check your answers with the answers in the back of the book.

8.5 Combine Words to Form Sentences

Read the words in the lists below:

Dawn	Boston
Laura	Austin
Lawrence	Saginaw
Walter	Auckland
Paul	Salt Lake City

Remember the simple past of the following irregular verbs?

bring _____   buy _____   catch _____

fight _____   think _____   teach _____

seek _____

Write questions and answers using these verbs and words from the list.

Example: Did Laura think of Paul in Boston?
No. She thought of Walter.

_____

_____

_____

_____

_____

_____

_____

_____

_____

8.6 Vocabulary

Study the meanings of the following words:

unfortunately: unluckily

cough: a rough noise from the throat, made especially when a
person has a cold

although: even if, in spite of the fact that

fall: (1) the season after summer; (2) to drop unexpectedly from a
high position to a lower one

spring: (1) the season before summer; (2) a place where water
comes out of the earth and forms a pool

Complete the sentences using the words above:

1. She felt warm, _____ the weather was cold.

2. At Hot _____s, Arkansas, hot water comes out of the
ground.

3. Be careful! Don't _____ !

4. _____ , he lost all of his money at Las Vegas.

5. When we catch a cold, we often _____ .

6. In Vermont, the leaves are beautiful in the _____ .

Answers are in the back of the book.

Look for these words in the story on the next page.

8.7 Read

Paul

Paul loved to be near the water all year long. One windy fall day, he was walking near a spring. Unfortunately, Paul had caught a bad cold, and he started coughing so hard that he fell. As he was falling, poor Paul stopped breathing and died. Although the police found his body in the spring, he had died in the fall.

Find 10 <u>different</u> words with the /ɔ/ sound in the story. List them below:

Check your answers with the answers in the back of the book.

8.8 Speak

Ask and answer these questions with a partner:

1. When did Paul love to be near the water?
2. Where was he walking one windy, fall day?
3. What unfortunate thing happened to him?
4. Why did he fall?
5. Who found his body?
6. What is the worst way to die? Why?

8.9 Listen and Say

There **was** a young **fellow** named **Paul**

Who **fell** in the **spring** in the **fall**.

'T would have **been** a sad **thing**

Had he **died** in the **spring**,

But he **didn't** — he **died** in the **fall**.

Practice repeating the limerick line by line. Notice the stress on the underlined syllables of the content words. Also notice how the syllables of a phrase (a group of words) are spoken as if the phrase were one word. Practice saying these phrases:

ayoung<u>fell</u>ow	whata<u>shame</u>
inthe<u>spring</u>	outof<u>bed</u>
asad<u>thing</u>	onher<u>head</u>
inthe<u>fall</u>	fromthe<u>Rhine</u>
tohis<u>granny</u>	inthe<u>sky</u>
whata<u>pleasure</u>	forthem<u>selves</u>
inthe<u>sun</u>	

Memorize the limerick.

8.10 Expansion

We know that *fall* and *spring* are the names of seasons of the year. Fall is the season between summer and winter and occurs during the months of September, October, and November. Spring is the season between winter and summer and occurs during the months of March, April, and May. These words can have other meanings, too. *Spring* can also mean a body of water. It can also mean to jump or move forward suddenly. *Fall* has many meanings, especially when used with a particle.

Fill in the blank spaces with the letter of the right "fall" word used with a particle:

1. Be careful! Don't _____ that old trick.	A. fall back
2. We tried hard to reach our goal, but unfortunately we _____.	B. fall back on
3. If this doesn't work, we can always _____ the old method.	C. falling behind
4. I think this problem _____ the category of "very difficult."	D. fell flat
	E. fall for
5. Our profits are _____. We need to take a new approach.	F. falling off
6. We're not making any progress. Let's _____ and start over.	G. falling out
	H. fell short
7. No, we weren't successful. We _____ on our faces.	I. fallen through
8. They've had a _____ , and they're not speaking to each other.	J. falls under
9. I'm not keeping up. I'm _____ .	Classification
10. Our plans have _____ . We can't go.	

8.11 Read — Letters to Paul

Dear Paul,

Where are you now? Are you in heaven or in the other place? Anyway, wherever you are, what are you doing? Please write to me soon. In the meantime, remember to watch your step.

Sincerely,

Audrey, Auckland

Dear Paul,

I am a fortune teller who can foresee the future. I want to warn you to be careful because I see a spring and a fall for you, and I see water. I hope that this letter doesn't arrive too late.

All my best,

Laura, Australia

Dear Paul,

I'm sorry you died. I borrowed some money from you, but now how can I return it? So, I've decided to send you beautiful flowers instead of paying you back. Farewell.

Sincerely,

Oliver, Milwaukee

8.12 Write

Write a letter of your own to Paul. Share it with the class.

Dear Paul,

8.13 Homonym

What happens when a lion stops moving?

HINT: A lion's feet are called its paws.

Notes:

UNIT 9
Joe

Vowel Focus: /ow/ **as in J<u>oe</u>**

Joe'd rather have fingers than toes;
He'd rather have ears than a nose;
And as for his hair,
He's glad that it's there.
He'll be awfully sad when it goes.

9.2 Spelling

The sound /ow/ is usually written with the letters *o, o...e, oa,* and *ow:*

> *o* as in *only*
> *o...e* as in *nose*
> *oa* as in *boat*
> *ow* as in *row*

Examples (listen or read and say):

One syllable: **so   low   coat   rose**
Two syllables: **o** cean   **mo** tor   **Cho** pin   **Mo** zart
Three syllables: e **mo** tion   com **pos** er
Four syllables: **O** kla **ho** ma   ap **pro** pri ate   Na **pol** e on

Add some words of your own in the spaces below:

1 Syllable	*2 Syllables*	*3 Syllables*	*4 Syllables*

Note: Other spellings are: *oe* as in *toes, ough* as in *doughnut* or *although.*

9.3 Compare Sounds and Words

Listen to and practice saying the sounds below:

/a/	/ow/
want	won't
hop	hope
calm	comb
sock	soak
rob	robe
Sol	soul, sole
Spock	spoke
clock	cloak
rod	road
cod	code
mop	mope

Practice reading and saying the following sentences aloud:

1. She put a **clock** in her **cloak.**
2. **Sol** won't tell a **soul.**
3. There's a **rod** on the **road.**
4. I **want** to, but I **won't.**
5. Dr. **Spock spoke.**

Can you make some other silly pair sentences?

_____

_____

_____

_____

_____

_____

9.4 Vowel Hunt

Identify the vowel sound /ow/ in these newspaper ads:

Treasure Trove
Of Fossils
Turns Up
In the Gobi

holly hunter   harvey keitel   sam neill
the Piano
a jane campion film
a jan chapman production
LOEW'S 34TH ST. SHOWPLACE

FOOLPROOF STRATEGIES FOR
SUCCESSFULLY NEGOTIATING YOUR
WAY THROUGH EVERY SITUATION

Check your answers with the answers in the back of the book.

9.5 Combine Words to Form Sentences

Read the words in the lists below:

Joan	soloist	Omaha
Tony	hostess	Oklahoma
Rhoda	broker	Rome
Joey	soldier	Tokyo
Omar	motorist	Okinawa

Write sentences using the words in the list above and the adjective at the beginning of each line.

Example: **boastful.** Joan spoke with her boastful broker in Tokyo.

old _____

bold _____

hopeful _____

outspoken _____

nosy _____

sociable _____

open-minded _____

overconfident _____

9.6 Vocabulary

Study the meanings of the following words:

suppose: believe
prefer: like better
emotional: having strong feelings
hold onto: keep; don't lose
heartbroken: filled with sadness
bald: having no hair
(woul)d rather: prefer

Complete the sentences using the words above:

1. Joe says he _____ fingers to toes.

2. He also says he'd _____ have ears than a nose.

3. Joe is _____ about keeping his hair. He wants to _____ it.

4. I _____ he'll be _____ if he becomes _____ .

Look for these words in the story on the next page.

9.7 Read

Joe

I suppose that Joe is joking when he says that he prefers fingers to toes and ears to a nose. But I don't think he's joking about his hair. He's very emotional about holding onto it. He'll be heart-broken if his hair goes. Joe hopes that when he gets older, he won't become bald. I don't blame him.

Find 13 <u>different</u> words with the /ow/ sound in the story. List them below:

Check your answers with the answers in the back of the book.

9.8 Speak

Ask and answer these questions with a partner:

1. What does Joe prefer to toes?
2. Would he rather have ears or a nose?
3. How does he feel about his hair now?
4. How will he feel if he loses his hair?
5. What do you think about baldness?
6. Which would you prefer: to be deaf or to be blind?

9.9 Listen and Say

Joe'd **rather** have **fingers** than **toes**;

He'd **rather** have **ears** than a **nose**;

And **as** for his **hair**,

He's **glad** that it's **there**.

He'll be **awfully** **sad** when it **goes**.

Practice repeating the limerick line by line. Notice the stress on the underlined syllables of the content words.

Practice saying the limerick by substituting I or Flo for Joe:

I'd rather …

Flo'd rather …

Memorize the limerick.

9.10 Expansion

Rather has three meanings:

1. With *would*, it means "to prefer." It is like a modal auxiliary, and the *would* is usually contracted in speech — for example:

   I'*d rather* go now.

2. It can mean "instead of" or "in place of," and it is used with *than*.

3. It is also like *very*, but not as strong. It is similar in meaning to *quite*.

Read the following sentences and decide which meaning of rather each one uses:

1. I'm <u>rather</u> tired.
2. I'd <u>rather</u> have long hair than short hair.
3. Let's phone him at 7:00 <u>rather</u> than 8:00.

Write sentences of your own to show the different meanings of rather:

_____

_____

_____

_____

_____

_____

_____

_____

_____

_____

9.11 Read — Letters to Joe

Dear Joe,

I think you are rather funny.

Somebody told me that you prefer fingers and ears to toes and a nose. I think that maybe you like to play the piano and listen to yourself. That's because you prefer your fingers and your ears.

As for your hair, don't worry. Now there are a lot of things you can do. For example, if you don't like wigs, that's not a problem. Hair technology is very advanced, and you can get a hair transplant. I'm sure you'll be fine.

Sincerely,

Lowell
Oklahoma City

Dear Joe,

Hi, honey. Don't feel sad. You are my sunshine. If you become bald, I'll still love you.

My grandmother taught me not to judge a person from the outside. Also, don't you know that many famous men were bald. For example, the former president of Korea was bald, and his hairstyle was very popular in Korea. And how about President Eisenhower?

Don't worry. Be happy.

Your sweetheart,

Mona
Lowell

9.12 Write

Write a letter of your own to Joe. Share it with
the class.

Dear Joe,

9.13 Homonym

What happened to the evil king?

HINT: The seat that a king sits on is called a *throne*.

Notes:

Word Search

Find 24 words with the /ow/ sound.

A Wordsearch Puzzle for Joe

M	O	L	B	Z	P	O	C	K	E	T	W	T
R	N	S	O	E	E	W	A	N	T	O	A	D
M	O	F	P	W	L	M	X	S	R	O	T	O
O	S	S	L	O	M	O	O	G	B	R	O	U
T	S	O	E	O	K	O	W	T	E	Y	L	T
I	O	G	C	L	W	E	T	S	I	N	D	M
O	C	C	U	K	Y	B	O	O	A	O	P	O
N	N	O	K	L	M	P	F	E	R	B	N	D
V	S	A	N	O	M	K	C	L	C	Z	J	E
B	O	O	C	O	C	O	D	P	H	O	N	R
S	H	J	C	O	V	A	J	P	O	O	A	N
C	G	J	L	K	O	W	O	N	T	L	P	T
U	E	C	D	R	D	F	T	O	E	S	E	E

UNIT 10
Roy

Vowel Focus: /oy/ **as in R__oy__**

There was a young fellow from Boise
Who at times was exceedingly noisy.
So his friends' joy increased
When he moved way back East
To what people in Brooklyn call "Joise."

10.2 Spelling

The sound /oy/ is usually written with the letters *oi* or *oy:*

> *oi* as in *noise, soil, choice, coin, avoid*
> *oy* as in *enjoy, employ, royal*

Examples (listen or read and say):

One syllable: **point**   **toy**   **spoil**
Two syllables: **boy** cott   **poi** son   **oy** ster   **loi** ter
Three syllables: cor du **roy**   **bois** ter ous
Four syllables: un em **ploy** ment   **mois** tur iz er

Add some words of your own in the spaces below:

1 Syllable	*2 Syllables*	*3 Syllables*	*4 Syllables*
_____	_____	_____	_____
_____	_____	_____	_____
_____	_____	_____	_____
_____	_____	_____	_____
_____	_____	_____	_____
_____	_____	_____	_____
_____	_____	_____	_____
_____	_____	_____	_____

Notes: 1. People from Brooklyn, a part of New York City, are famous for their special pronunciation of certain sounds. The /ər/ sound, as in *Ursula,* is pronounced more like /oy/. So a *bird* in most of the U.S. is a "boid" in Brooklyn, and *New Jersey* is "New Joise." 2. And the capital of Idaho is pronounced to rhyme with *noisy,* not *noise.*

10.3 Compare Sounds and Words

Listen to and practice saying the sounds below:

/ey/	/iy/	/ay/	/oy/
fail	feel	file	foil
say	see	sigh	soy
ail	eel	aisle	oil
tale	teal	tile	toil
lane	lean	line	loin

What's the word?

a kind of sauce   _____

the opposite of pass   _____

understand   _____

work hard   _____

a passage between seats   _____

breathe out with a sound   _____

metallic paper   _____

a snake-like fish   _____

a story   _____

10.4 Vowel Hunt

Identify the vowel sound /oy/ in these newspaper ads:

AT&T
Your True Choice

TOYOTA 4Runner
"I love what you do for me"

R&H Voyages
A tradition of proven performance since 1979

Royal Caribbean

'Bill Moyers's Journal'
'Poet Laureate Rita Dove'
PBS, tonight at 9.
(Channel 13 in New York.)

Check your answers with the answers in the back of the book.

10.5 Combine Words to Form Sentences

Read the words in the lists below:

Roy	join	Detroit
Joyce	employ	Boise
Troy	boil	Troy
Lloyd	avoid	Illinois
Toya	toil	Des Moines
Moira	destroy	Sheboygan

Combine words from these lists to form sentences.

Example: Roy joined a union in Detroit.

_____

_____

_____

_____

_____

_____

_____

_____

_____

_____

10.6 Vocabulary

Study the meanings of the following words:

boisterous: noisy and rowdy
recognize: know and remember
avoid: stay away from
rejoice: celebrate, feel joyful
joy: happiness
roots: original home

Complete the sentences using the words above:

1. When the weather is hot, you should _____ drinking alcohol.

2. Although he lived in the North, his _____ were in the South.

3. Some people become _____ at a party.

4. There was great _____ when the war ended, and everyone _____ .

5. I didn't _____ you because you changed your hairstyle.

Write a few sentences with the words above:

_____

_____

_____

_____

_____

Look for these words in the story on the next page.

10.7 Read

Roy

Roy had lived in Boise, Idaho, for many years. He was very noisy, and everyone recognized his loud voice. In fact, Roy made so much noise that his friends avoided seeing him. When Roy decided to move, they rejoiced. When people asked where he was going, Roy revealed his Brooklyn roots. He said he was leaving "Ol' Boise" and moving to "New Joise."

Find 8 <u>different</u> words with the /oy/ sound in the story. List them below:

Check your answers with the answers in the back of the book.

10.8 Speak

Ask and answer these questions with a partner:

1. Where had Roy lived for many years?
2. What kind of person was he?
3. What did his friends begin to do?
4. When did they rejoice?
5. How did Roy show his Brooklyn roots?

10.9 Listen and Say

There **was** a young **fellow** from **Boise**,

Who at **times** was **exceedingly noisy**.

So his **friends'** joy **increased**

When he **moved** way back **East**

To what **people** in **Brooklyn**

call "**Joise**."

Practice repeating the limerick line by line.
Try saying it a few times by saying only
the words in boldface type. Be sure to
emphasize the underlined syllables – e.g.,
"exCEEDingly."

Memorize the limerick.

10.10 Expansion

Some verbs in English are always followed by gerunds (verb + ing). *Enjoy* and *avoid* are two of these verbs. *Enjoy* means to get happiness from something. *Avoid* means to stay away from something.

> *Example:* We **enjoy** listening to music, but we **avoid** listening to loud noises.

What do you enjoy doing?

1. _____
2. _____
3. _____
4. _____
5. _____

What do you avoid doing?

1. _____
2. _____
3. _____
4. _____
5. _____

Some other common verbs that are usually followed only by gerunds are: *admit, consider, delay, deny, discuss, dislike, finish, keep, mind, miss, practice, quit, recall, resent, suggest, understand.*

Can you use the verbs above in a sentence about Roy?

10.11 Read — Letters to Roy

Dear Roy,

How are you? I think that maybe you make so much noise because you don't hear very well. If you are a little deaf, you should see a doctor. My other advice is this: When you make new friends in New Jersey, try to be quieter when you are with them. Otherwise, you may have to move again.

Good luck in your new home.

Sincerely,

Doyle
Troy

Dear Roy,

We're sorry you moved to New Jersey. Without you around, Boise is so boring. We need you and miss your boisterous laugh. If you would consider returning, we'll send a plane ticket and help you find employment.

Love,

The McCoys
Not-so-noisy Boise

Date: Thoisday, 29 February
From: Floyd <fboyle@boise.com>
To: Roy <royboy@jersey.net>
Subject: Staying in touch

Hi Roy --

I think I'll enjoy this way of staying in touch.
Don't call; just hit reply.

Hope you like New Joise more than Boise.

Floyd Boyle

Can you write an E-mail to Roy?

10.12 Write

Write a letter of your own to Roy. Share it with the class.

Dear Roy,

10.13 Homonym

Why can't visitors enter the palace?

HINT: One meaning of *roil* is "to irritate or bother."

Notes:

Review

Without looking back, review Units 6–10 by yourself, with a partner, or with a small group:

- First, tell each character's story.
- Next, try to say the limerick.
- When you have finished, look back at the five units.
- Finally, decidewhich limerick you like best and why. Then discuss your ideas with others.

UNIT 11
Brooke

Vowel Focus: /u/ as in Br<u>oo</u>ke

There was a young girl from Asturias
Whose antics were frantic and furious.
She used to throw eggs
At her grandmother's legs,
A habit unpleasant and curious.

11.2 Spelling

The sound /u/ is usually written with the letters *oo* or *u*.

oo as in *good, look, took, book*
u as in *full, pull*

Examples (listen or read and say):

One syllable: **look   took   book   wood   full**
Two syllables: **cook** ie   **pud** ding   **cush** ion   **butch** er
Three syllables: neigh bor **hood**   **good-look** ing
Four syllables: mis un der **stood**

Add some words of your own in the spaces below:

1 Syllable	*2 Syllables*	*3 Syllables*	*4 Syllables*
_____	_____	_____	_____
_____	_____	_____	_____
_____	_____	_____	_____
_____	_____	_____	_____
_____	_____	_____	_____
_____	_____	_____	_____
_____	_____	_____	_____
_____	_____	_____	_____
_____	_____	_____	_____

Note: Other spellings are: *ou* as in *could, would,* and *should; o* as in *woman* and *wolf*.

11.3 Compare Sounds and Words

Listen to and practice saying the sounds below:

/u/	/uw/
soot	suit
full	fool
stood	stewed
Toots	toots

Practice reading these silly sentences aloud:

He stood there and stewed about the soot on his suit.
Ghouls do foolish things when the moon is full.
Her pocketbook was full of cookies and Tootsie Rolls.
Toots doesn't give a hoot about tooting a flute.
She took a look at the book and called it crude and lewd.
After one look, he was so shook up he couldn't keep his cool.

Look these up and cook up some sentences of your own:

good-looking   hood   hook   wood

_____

_____

_____

_____

_____

_____

_____

_____

11.4 Vowel Hunt

Identify the vowel sound /u/ in these newspaper ads:

GOODY GOT IT.

NEW YORK
ANTIQUARIAN
BOOK
FAIR

**Wool Berber
for less than
wholesale.
At ABC.**

BROOKS ATKINSON THEATRE

Check your answers with the answers in the back of the book.

11.5 Combine Words to Form Sentences

Read the words in the lists below:

Brooke	footballs	Brooklyn
Woodrow	cookbooks	Europe
Cookie	cushions	Burundi
Wolf	pullovers	Zurich
Captain Cook	woodpeckers	Surinam

Combine words from these lists to form sentences.

Example: Captain Cook collected woodpeckers
from Surinam.

_____

_____

_____

_____

_____

_____

_____

_____

_____

_____

11.6 Vocabulary

Study the meanings of the following words:

antics: playful behavior
furious: wild and angry
frantic: wild and frightened
habit: usual, customary behavior
curious: strange, odd, peculiar

Complete the sentences using the words above:

1. She'll be _____ if I'm late again.

2. There was a _____ rush to get off the airplane.

3. I'm in the _____ of getting up at six o'clock.

4. Isn't that a _____ sight!

5. Monkeys are well known for their amusing _____ .

Write some sentences with the words above:

_____

_____

_____

_____

_____

_____

_____

Look for these words in the story on the next page.

11.7 Read

Brooke

Brooke was a young girl who lived in Asturias. Most of the time she was a very gentle person. She loved to wear wool clothes and sit on soft cushions. She enjoyed eating chocolate pudding and cookies. She was a good girl most of the time. However, when she got angry, she quickly became furious. She did wild, crazy things, such as throwing eggs. One day she threw eggs at her poor grandmother's legs. As she threw the eggs, she knew that she shouldn't throw them. She knew that she should break this very bad habit. She tried frantically to change. Alas! She just couldn't stop.

Find 10 <u>different</u> words with the /u/ sound in the story. List them below:

Check your answers with the answers in the back of the book.

11.8 Speak

Ask and answer these questions with a partner:

1. Where did Brooke live?
2. What things did Brooke like?
3. What happened when she lost her temper?
4. What's your opinion of Brooke's antics?
5. How do you deal with anger?

Say and discuss the meaning of the following lines from the poem "The Road Not Taken," by Robert Frost. These are from the first and last stanzas of the poem.

Two roads diverged in a yellow wood,

And sorry I could not travel both

And be one traveler, long I stood

And looked down one as far as I could

…

Two roads diverged in a wood, and I —

I took the one less traveled by,

And that has made all the difference.

11.9 Listen and Say

There **was** a young **girl** from **Asturias,**

Whose **antics** were **frantic** and **furious.**

She **used** to throw **eggs**

At her **grandmother's legs,**

A **habit unpleasant** and **curious.**

Practice repeating the limerick line by line until you have memorized it. Then pair up with a classmate and take turns asking the questions below and answering with lines from the limerick.

Example: **A:** Where was she from?
B: From Asturias.

Who was Brooke?
How did she behave?
What did she throw?
At what did she throw them?
What kind of behavior was this?

With a partner, talk about times when you have been frantic or furious.

11.10 Expansion

Some people *lose their temper* when they are very angry, and do or say unpleasant things. Others are able to control their temper and stay calm.

When the young girl of Asturias lost her temper, she threw things. She couldn't control her temper.

Some other things that people do when they lose their temper are: shout and shake their fists.

Some other things that people do to control their temper are: count to ten and take a deep breath.

What do you do when you lose your temper?

What do you do to control your temper?

Check out the meanings of these other verbs and idioms for emotions that often lead to losing one's temper. Try using them in a sentence about Brooke or yourself.

abhor	aggravate	agitate	irritate
annoy	antagonize	bother	burn up
detest	fume	hate	hurt

blow one's top	fit to be tied
hot and bothered	make a scene
be teed off [slang]	be pissed off [vulgar]

_____

_____

_____

_____

_____

_____

11.11 Read — Letters to Brooke

Dear Brooke,

When you throw eggs at your grandmother's legs, don't forget that eggs cost money. I think it's a wasteful habit, and a messy one, too. Who cleans up the mess?

Sincerely,

Ms. Goodman
Sherbrooke

Dear Brooke,

I think I know why you used to throw eggs at your granny. It was because she cooked eggs every day: omelets, fried eggs, scrambled eggs, boiled eggs, and so on. Didn't you ever tell her that you hated eggs?

Maybe you should buy her a new cookbook.

Sincerely,

Woody
Brooklyn

Dear Brooke,

Look! If you must throw eggs, why don't you cook them first. If you just took a little time, then you might even cool off and take a good look at yourself and what you're doing.

If I were you, I would get a good book about psychology and read it; that could help you with your problem. Or maybe you should chop wood when you feel this strange mood coming on. That would relieve tension.

Good luck,

Dr. Fulton Cooke
Worcester

11.12 Write

What do you want to say to Brooke? Write a letter of your own and share it with the class.

Dear Brooke,

11.13 Homonym

Who'd take the bull by the horns?

HINT: Mr. Wood is a brave man.

Notes:

UNIT 12
Louis

Vowel Focus: /uw/ as in L<u>ou</u>is

Louis made quite a to-do
When he found a small mouse in his stew.
Said the waiter, "Don't shout
And wave it about,
Or the rest will be wanting one too."

12.2 Spelling

The sound /uw/ is usually written with the letters *oo, u, ou, o, u...e.*

> *oo* as in *soon, afternoon, food*
> *u* as in *truth*
> *ou* as in *through, you*
> *o* as in *do, who, movie*
> *u...e* as in *rule*

Examples (listen or read and say):

One syllable: **school   spoon   group**
Two syllables: **cuck oo   fool** ish
Three syllables: **lu** na tic   in **clud** ed
Four syllables: re vo **lu** tion   com **mu** ni cate

Add some words of your own in the spaces below:

1 Syllable	2 Syllables	3 Syllables	4 Syllables
——————	——————	——————	——————
——————	——————	——————	——————
——————	——————	——————	——————
——————	——————	——————	——————
——————	——————	——————	——————
——————	——————	——————	——————
——————	——————	——————	——————
——————	——————	——————	——————

Note: There are several other spellings for /uw/: *oo...e* as in *choose, loose; o...e* as in *lose; ew* as in *jewel, flew, new; ui* as in *suit, fruit, juice.*

12.3 Compare Sounds and Words

Compare the vowel sounds in these words.
Which word doesn't belong? (Read across.)

1. pool	soon	boot	look
2. do	to	no	who
3. so	smooth	clue	brew
4. move	put	goose	juice
5. truth	rude	booth	blood
6. blew	crew	sew	flew
7. cool	cook	rule	due

Make your own list of sound pairs.

Example: pull — pool

/u/ /uw/

1. _____ _____

2. _____ _____

3. _____ _____

4. _____ _____

5. _____ _____

Create sentences using your pairs.

Example: I pulled her from the pool.

_____

_____

_____

_____

_____

_____

12.4 Vowel Hunt

Identify the vowel sound /uw/ in these newspaper ads:

AMERICA'S #1 MOVIE
One Flew Over
The Cuckoo's Nest

bloomingdale's
for
shoes

HOOP DREAMS
2:00, 5:35, 8:45
"TWO THUMBS UP!"
SISKEL & EBERT

MITSUBISHI
The word is getting around.

Check your answers with the answers in the back of the book.

12.5 Combine Words to Form Sentences

Read the words in the lists below:

Stuart	Peru
Ruth	Pusan
Julia	Massachusetts
Susan	Jerusalem
Luke	Chattanooga
Rudy	Duluth
Brutus	Cooperstown
Truman	Baku
June	Honolulu

Combine words from these lists to form sentences.

Example: Stuart grew up in Chattanooga.

_____

_____

_____

_____

_____

_____

_____

_____

_____

_____

12.6 Vocabulary

Study the meanings of the following words:

stew: a meal of meat, chicken, or fish and vegetables, cooked in a
liquid
include: to have as part of something, contain
nutritious: food that is good for the body
to-do: a state of confusion, a noisy demonstration
wave: to move from side to side
about: around, from one place to another

Complete the sentences using the words above:

1. Vegetables are _____ .

2. Why did he make a big _____ ?

3. A dish that _____ meat and vegetables is called
   a _____ .

4. When he saw the mouse, the waiter said, "Don't
   _____ it _____ ."

Write some sentences with the words above:

_____

_____

_____

_____

_____

_____

_____

Look for these words in the story on the next page.

12.7 Read

Louis

On a cool day in June, Louis went to a restaurant. He decided to have stew because stew includes nutritious foods. The waiter served the stew and Louis became truly angry because there was a mouse in it. He called the waiter in a loud voice and made a big to-do. The waiter said, "Shh." He told Louis to keep cool and asked him not to wave the mouse in the air. The waiter said that if they saw it, the other diners would choose to have a mouse in their stew, too. Louis thought the waiter was foolish.

Find 12 <u>different</u> words with the /uw/ sound in the story.

Check your answers with the answers in the back of the book.

12.8 Speak

Ask and answer these questions with a partner:

1. Where was Louis?
2. Why did he make a to-do?
3. What two things did the waiter tell him not to do?
4. Who else would want a mouse stew?
5. What would you do if you were Louis?

12.9 Listen and Say

Lou̱is made qu̱ite a to-ḏo

When he foṵnd a small moṵse in his stew̱,

Said the waṵiter, "Don't shoṵt

And waṵve it aboṵt,

Or the res̱t will be waṉting one toọ."

Pair up with a classmate and practice repeating the limerick line by line until you have memorized it. Take turns answering questions about each line and answering with lines from the limerick.

Example: **A:** Who made a to-do?
           B: Louis made quite a to-do.

           A: What did he find?
           B: A mouse in his stew.

Then do a short role-play together, acting out the scene.

12.10 Expansion

Hugo,
the Musical Moose

You may have noticed that in some cases the /uw/ sound is preceded by a /y/ sound, but a *y* does not appear in the spelling of the word. *Hugo,* for example, is pronounced /hyuwgow/, and not /huwgow/. *Musical* is /myuwzikəl/, but *moose* is /muws/. The /yuw/ sound will be the focus of the next unit.

In the list of words that follows, all the words that are pronounced with y + uw are underlined. Pronounce them.

crew	you	few	clue	true	cue
music	moose	move	mute	argue	grew
union	view	blue	due/dew	tool	excuse
sue	spoon	shoe	bureau	cute	use
curious	brew	cucumber	voodoo	flew	~~blue~~ blew
June	loose	new	pure	rule	stew

Now list and pronounce the words above that have the /uw/ sound:

B	blue, brew	J	_____	R	_____
C	crew, clue	K	_____	S	_____
D	~~none~~ dew, due	L	_____	T	_____
F	_____	M	_____	V	_____
G	_____	N	_____	W	_____
H	_____	P	_____	Z	_____

12.11 Read — Letters to Louis

Dear Louis,

I wouldn't like to find a mouse in my stew, and I think that other diners wouldn't choose to have a mouse in their stew, either. The sly waiter told you that story to fool you, and you were right when you became angry.

I hope that you will never be foolish enough to let anyone convince you of something that is untrue.

Sincerely,

Rudy, Bloomfield

Dear Louis,

I'm sorry about what happened to you. I know that you are very angry now, but don't be mad at the waiter. It wasn't his fault. It was the chef's fault.

Did you know that the mouse is a delicacy in some countries, and some people eat moose. Although I think it's fun to try different foods, I would not try to eat a mouse, but I would eat a kangaroo. I understand your reaction. Let's have dinner together some time, but <u>not</u> in <u>that</u> restaurant.

Sincerely,

Bruno, Broome, Australia

12.12 Write

What do you want to say to Louis? Write a letter of your own and share it with the class.

Dear Louis,

12.13 Homonym

Where did the foolish bird fly?

HINT: The opening in a chimney where the smoke comes out is called a flue.

Notes:

UNIT 13
Ulysses

Vowel Focus: /yuw/ as in <u>U</u>lysses

Ulysses, a mule from Cathay,
Played an old ukelele all day.
When the duke ordered quiet,
The mule didn't buy it
And played his old uke anyway.

13.2 Spelling

The sound /yuw/ is usually written with the letters *u, u...e,* and *ew.*

u as in *unit*
u...e as in *useful*
ew as in *few*

Other spellings are: *eau* as in *beauty, ie* as in *view.*

Examples (listen or read and say):

One syllable: **hue   pure   cute   fuse**
Two syllables: ex **cuse   fu** ture
Three syllables: **cu** cum ber   **u** ni corn   **u** ni form
Four syllables: **u** ni ver sal   un **u** su al

/yuw/ often occurs when *u* is the first letter of a word and after these consonants made with the lips and teeth:

| **b** | beauty | **p** | pupil | **f** | fuse |
| **v** | view | **m** | music | | |

and these consonants that are made in the back of the mouth:

| **c** | cute | **g** | argue | **h** | human |

Some Americans also pronounce *u* as /yuw/ before the consonant *d* as in *due, duke.*

Add some words of your own in the spaces below:

1 Syllable	*2 Syllables*	*3 Syllables*	*4 Syllables*
_____	_____	_____	_____
_____	_____	_____	_____
_____	_____	_____	_____
_____	_____	_____	_____

13.3 Compare Sounds and Words

Compare the vowel sounds in these words.

/uw/	/yuw/
whose	hues
fool	fuel
mood	mewed
who	Hugh
coot	cute
moot	mute

What's the word?

1. A man's name _____

2. It produces energy when it burns _____

3. Colors _____

4. Feeling, spirit, or tone _____

5. Question words _____ and _____

6. A stupid person _____

7. Unable to speak _____

8. Pretty or attractive _____

Others:

A sound made by a cat	*mew*
A bird like a duck	*coot*
A meaningless discussion	*moot*

13.4 Vowel Hunt

Here are some examples of newspaper ads that use the /yuw/ sound. Read the ads and list all the words that use that sound. Find other examples and prepare to share them with the class.

BEAUTY AND THE BEAST

A NEW MUSICAL

The most beautiful love story ever told comes to life on Broadway

J&R **COMPUTER WORLD**

(Thurs. demo)
New York, NY
1 (800) 221-8180

MUTUAL FUNDS

Check your answers with the answers in the back of the book.

13.5 Combine Words to Form Sentences

Read the words in the lists below:

Eugene	Cuba
Eudora	The Yucatan
Beulah	Uruguay
Hugh	The United States
Hugo	Ukraine

Combine words from each column to form sentences with usually.

Example: Eugene usually goes to Cuba in the winter for vacation.

_____

_____

_____

_____

_____

_____

_____

_____

_____

13.6 Vocabulary

Study the meanings of the following words:

reputation: an opinion held by others about someone or something; what a person is known for

stubborn: unwilling to change

to be no exception: not different

contribute: to give something of value to someone or something

ukelele: a small musical instrument somewhat like a guitar

amused: entertained, pleased, charmed

Complete the sentences using the words above:

1. Will you _____ some money to the museum?

2. It would be _____ing to see a mule play a mkelele.

3. There are no _____ s to this rule.

4. Mules have a _____ for being _____.

5. A _____ has only four strings.

Write some sentences with the words above:

_____

_____

_____

_____

_____

_____

_____

Look for these words in the story on the next page.

13.7 Read

Ulysses

In the Dukedom of Eureka, within the Kingdom of Cathay, there lived a mule named Ulysses. Mules have a reputation for being stubborn, and Ulysses was no exception. He refused to change his usual habits.

Eureka was ruled by a duke. The duke loved art, and he contributed a fabulous collection to the museum. Although he loved art, the duke hated music.

The duke was a very powerful ruler, and everyone was afraid of him, except Ulysses. He loved music and usually played his ukelele all day. The duke was not amused. He ordered Ulysses to stop. Ulysses was stubborn and refused to obey the order. After all, he was a mule.

What do you think happened to him?

Find 13 different words with the /uw/ sound in the story. List them below:

Check your answers with the answers in the back of the book.

13.8 Speak

Ask and answer these questions with a partner:

1. Where did Ulysses live?
2. What reputation do mules have?
3. Who else lived in Eureka?
4. What did the duke do? And what did Ulysses do?
5. What do you think happened to Ulysses?

Discuss music with a partner or a group. Talk about your favorite musical instruments, performers, songs, and compositions.

13.9 Listen and Say

Ulysses, a **mule** from **Cathay**,
Played an **old** ukelele all **day**.
When the **duke** ordered **quiet**,
The **mule** didn't **buy** it
And **played** his old **uke** anyway.

Pair up with a classmate and practice repeating the limerick line by line until you have memorized it. Take turns answering questions about each line and answering with lines from the limerick.

In this limerick, *to buy* means *to believe* or *accept*.

Talk about something that you don't buy.

Example: Do you buy this story?

Then do a short role-play together, acting out the scene, with your ending to the story.

13.10 Expansion

In a dictionary, pronunciation is shown in parentheses as a phonetic equivalent after each word.

Look up the following words with the /yuw/ sound in your dictionary. Copy the phonetic equivalent after each word.

mutual	_____	humorous	_____
cupid	_____	accumulate	_____
mute	_____	futile	_____
feud	_____	municipal	_____
fuel	_____	impunity	_____

The /u/ sound and the /ə/ sound are also sometimes pronounced as /yu/ and /yə/. Here are some examples. See if you can find others.

/yu/	/yə/
fury	accurate
bureau	regular
mural	angular
cure	executive
_____	_____
_____	_____
_____	_____
_____	_____

Also note that the letter *q* is always followed by the letter *u*. But this *u* is pronounced like a *w*. So, pronounce: *question, quarter, queen, quick, quote* — but be careful of *queue* and the name of the letter *q*. How are they pronounced?

13.11 Read — Letters to Ulysses

Dear Ulysses,

How are you? Are you still playing your ukelele?

I want to invite you and the duke to a Ukrainian restaurant where Ukrainian people like to sing and dance all day and night. When the duke sees everyone enjoying music so much, maybe he'll change his tune about your music. After all, music is the most beautiful form of communication.

I'll call you on Tuesday, and we can talk about it.

Sincerely,

Yuri
Union, Utah
(I used to live in Ukraine)

Dear Ulysses,

Hi. Because this letter is on tape, you can play your ukelele while you listen. Are you playing it now?

I had a simliar experience a long time ago. When I played the saxophone, my brother said that it was very noisy. He wanted me to stop playing. But I refused. We argued. Finally, when he couldn't stand the sound, he moved away.

I think that if the duke is not amused by the sound of your uke, maybe he will move to another place. I hear that Uruguay needs a new duke.

Your friend,

Hugo Unicorn
The Yucatan

13.12 Write

What do you want to say to Ulysses? Write a letter of your own and share it with the class.

Dear Ulysses,

13.13 Homonym

What did the mule's friend, the unicorn, say when the mule said, "Bah"?

HINT: A female sheep is a *ewe*.
Bah is an expression of scorn.
Baa is the sound a sheep makes.

___

Notes:

___

Ms. Brown

Vowel Focus: /aw/ **as in Ms. Br<u>ow</u>n**

A gal who weighed many an ounce
Used language I dare not pronounce
When a fellow unkind
Pulled her chair out from behind
Just to see (so he said) if she'd bounce.

14.2 Spelling

The sound /aw/ is usually written with the letters *ou* or *ow*.

> *ou* as in *south, about, thousand, found, pronounce, doubt*
> *ow* as in *how, vowel, crowd, flower, allow, powder, owl*

Examples (listen or read and say):

One syllable: **spouse**   **couch**   **sound**   **loud**
Two syllables: pro **nounce**   **foun** tain   dis **count**
Three syllables: al **low** ance   **out** stand ing   **foun** da tion
Four syllables: **moun** tain eer ing

Add some words of your own in the spaces below:

1 Syllable	*2 Syllables*	*3 Syllables*	*4 Syllables*
————	————	————	————
————	————	————	————
————	————	————	————
————	————	————	————
————	————	————	————
————	————	————	————
————	————	————	————
————	————	————	————

14.3 Compare Sounds and Words

Compare the vowel sounds in these words. Circle the words that have the /aw/ vowel sound.

gone	gown	grown	grain	groan	granny
doubt	dot	date	dote	dude	down
coach	catch	couch	crunch	chowder	crowd
flower	floor	flair	float	flat	flowed
pow-wow	powder	paw	proud	know-how	eyebrow
road	root	rout	round	rowed	rude

Practice reading the following sentences aloud:

Dot seems to doubt that the gown is gone.
Don fell down when Dawn moved the couch.
How now, brown cow?

Can you write your own silly sentences with /aw/ sounds?

_____

_____

_____

_____

_____

_____

14.4 Vowel Hunt

Here are some examples of newspaper ads that use the /aw/ sound. Read the ads and list all the words that use that sound. Find other examples and prepare to share them with the class.

**HOW TO SUCCEED
IN BUSINESS
WITHOUT
REALLY TRYING!**

MOUSE IN THE HOUSE

6 OUTER CRITICS
CIRCLE NOMINATIONS
including

**OUTSTANDING
MUSICAL
REVIVAL**

SHE LOVES ME

Check your answers with the answers in the back of the book.

14.5 Combine Words to Form Sentences

Read the words in the lists below:

Doctor Brown	accountant	in a crowd
Mr. Downey	clown	downtown
Mrs. Pound	announcer	in the shower
Ms. Fowler	counselor	on a mountain
Mr. & Mrs. South	bouncer	in a tower

Combine words from each column to form sentences.

Example: Ms. Fowler found a clown downtown.

_____

_____

_____

_____

_____

_____

_____

_____

_____

_____

14.6 Vocabulary

Study the meanings of the following words:

astounded: very surprised
mean: unkind, not nice, nasty
curious: eager to know
bounce: to come back up again, like a rubber ball

Complete the sentences using the words above:

1. Stealing their ball was a _____ thing to do.

2. They were _____ to hear they had won the lottery.

3. They like to _____ on the trampoline.

4. Successful students are usually _____ .

Write some sentences with the words above:

_____

_____

_____

_____

_____

_____

_____

_____

_____

_____

Look for these words in the story on the next page.

14.7 Read

Ms. Brown

Howard was astounded to see Ms. Brown in the house. Ms. Brown was as round as a ball. How many pounds and ounces could she weigh? Howard pulled the chair away when Ms. Brown tried to sit down. Howard said that he wasn't being mean. He explained that he was just curious to see if she'd bounce.

Find 10 <u>different</u> words with the /aw/ sound in the story. List them below:

Check your answers with the answers in the back of the book.

14.8 Speak

Ask and answer these questions with a partner:

1. Where was Howard?
2. Why was he astounded?
3. What question did he ask himself?
4. When did Howard pull the chair away?
5. What was he curious about?
6. What would you say to Howard if you were Ms. Brown's friend?

14.9 Listen and Say

A **gal** who weighed **many** an **ounce**

Used **language** I **dare** not **pronounce**

When a **fellow unkind**

Pulled her **chair** out from **behind**

Just to **see** (so he **said**) if she'd **bounce**.

Pair up with a classmate and practice repeating the limerick line by line until you have memorized it. Take turns answering questions about each line and answering with lines from the limerick. Use question words:

Who ... ?

How many ... ?

What kind ... ?

Why ... ?

What ... ?

Note: There are 16 ounces (oz.) in a pound (lb.). Just for fun: *ounce* is abbreviated to *oz.* How could you spell *pronounce* and *bounce*?

14.10 Expansion

An *abbreviation* is a shortened form of a word or phrase. There are three kinds of abbreviations in English:

1. The abbreviation is pronounced as the full word:

Abbreviation	Pronunciation and Word	
Dr.	/daktər/	Doctor
Mr.	/mistər/	Mister
oz.	/awns/	ounce(s)
lb.	/pawnd/	pound(s)

2. The abbreviation is pronounced with the names of the first letters of the words.

Abbreviation	Pronunciation	Complete Word/Phrase
B.A.	/biy ey/	Bachelor of Arts
M.D.	/em diy/	Medical Doctor
CBS	/ciy biy es/	Columbia Broadcasting System

3. The abbreviation is pronounced like a word:

Abbreviation	Pronunciation	Complete Phrase
UNESCO	/yuwnesko/	United Nations Educational, Scientific, and Cultural Organization
NASA	/næsə/	National Aeronautics and Space Administration

Can you abbreviate and say these words?

1. avenue _____
2. United Nations _____
3. National Broadcasting Company _____
4. department _____
5. Organization of Petroleum Exporting Countries _____
6. Master of Arts _____
7. Trans-World Airlines _____
8. street _____
9. junior _____

14.11 Read — Letters to Ms. Brown

Dear Ms. Brown,

How are you? Somebody told me what happened. I hope you weren't hurt. That Howard is a clown!

Let me give you some sound advice. The next time you plan to sit down, look around. Don't end up on the ground.

Your friend,

Dora Dow
Tarrytown

Dear Ms. Brown,

I think I know why you didn't bounce, even though you weigh so much. It is because you ate too much cheesecake and steak, instead of jello.

Please write to tell me if I'm right.

Yours truly,

Ms. Molly McCloud
Brownsville

14.12 Write

What do you want to say to Ms. Brown or to Howard? Or maybe you'd like to respond to Dora Dow or Molly McCloud. Write a letter of your own and share it with the class.

Dear _____ ,

14.13 Homonym

What did the pastry chef draw?

HINT: To make pastry, you need flour.

Notes:

UNIT 15
Ivy

Vowel Focus: /ay/ **as in** Ivy

There was a young lady from Niger,
Who smiled as she rode on a tiger.
They returned from the ride
With the lady inside,
And the smile on the face of the tiger.

15.2 Spelling

The sound /ay/ is usually written with the letters *i, i…e, y, y…e, igh,* and *ie.*

> *i* as in *I, find, behind*
> *i…e* as in *rice, kite*
> *y* as in *my, try*
> *y…e* as in *type, style*
> *igh* as in *might, sigh*
> *ie* as in *lie, die*

Examples (listen or read and say):

One syllable: **mice** **smile** **ride** **blind** **wife** **sight** **fly**
Two syllables: **ti** tle   be **side**   Ju **ly**   re **ply**   de **light**
Three syllables: **bi** cy cle   **li** bra ry   de **cid** ed
Four syllables: **psy** chol o gist   cap i tal **ize**

Add some words of your own in the spaces below:

1 Syllable	2 Syllables	3 Syllables	4 Syllables
_____	_____	_____	_____
_____	_____	_____	_____
_____	_____	_____	_____
_____	_____	_____	_____
_____	_____	_____	_____
_____	_____	_____	_____
_____	_____	_____	_____

Note: Other spellings are: *uy* as in *buy, ei* as in *height, ai* as in *aisle.*

15.3 Compare Sounds and Words

Compare the vowel sounds in these words.

sit	site	pill	pile
still	style	tip	type
rim	rhyme	fin	fine
hit	height	shin	shine
rid	ride	Tim	time
did	died	wit	white

Practice reading these sentences aloud:

1. We can't sit at this site.
2. Put a pill in the pile.
3. Tim has lots of time.
4. She still dresses in style.
5. That fish has a fine fin.

Make your own list of sound pairs.

Example: bit — bite

/i/	/ay/
1. _____	_____
2. _____	_____
3. _____	_____
4. _____	_____
5. _____	_____

Create a sentence or two using your pairs.

Example: Will it bite? It already bit.

_____

_____

_____

15.4 Vowel Hunt

Identify the vowel sound /ay/ in these newspaper ads.

ALL IN THE TIMING

"Utterly Delightful"
David Richards, WQXR Radio

"Intellectual Tomfoolery"
Ben Brantley, New York Times

"Snappy"
John Simon, New York Magazine

Written by
DAVID IVES

Directed by
**JASON
McCONNELL
BUZAS**

DiME.

Where to borrow.

Check your answers with the answers in the back of the book.

15.5 Combine Words to Form Sentences

Read the words in the lists below:

Ida	hiking	Guyana	five
Michael	diving	Iceland	nine
Simon	flying	Siberia	nineteen
Eileen	biking	Thailand	ninety-five
Riley	climbing	China	ninety-nine

Combine words from each column to form sentences.

Examples: Ida tried hiking in China in nineteen ninety-five.
Simon is flying to Iceland at nine.

_____

_____

_____

_____

_____

_____

_____

_____

_____

_____

15.6 Vocabulary

Study the meanings of the following words:

wild: not tame, undomesticated
frown: show disapproval with one's face
delighted: very pleased, happy
isolated: alone, separated from others
Niger: a country in Africa
spend: to pass time
jungle: a tropical forest

Complete the sentences using the words above:

1. She smiled because she was _____ , but other people
   _____ at her behavior.
2. There are many _____ animals in this _____ .
3. When you were in Africa, did you ever visit _____ ?
   Did you _____ any time in any _____ places
   like Agades?

Write some sentences with these words:

_____

_____

_____

_____

_____

_____

Look for these words in the story on the next page.

15.7 Read

Ivy

Ivy had spent her life in Niger, where there were
many wild animals. One fine Friday in July,
Ivy decided to ride on a tiger. She smiled with
delight as they started off. While Ivy smiled,
the tiger frowned. It was not at all delighted to
be carrying a passenger. Besides, it was quite
hungry. So, in an isolated part of the jungle,
where no one could watch, the tiger dined on the
lady. When it returned to town, Ivy was inside
the tiger, and she was not smiling. This time the
smile was on the face of the tiger.

**Find 22 <u>different</u> words with the /ay/ sound
in the story. List them below:**

Check your answers with the answers in the back of the book.

15.8 Speak

Ask and answer these questions with a partner:

1. Where was Ivy from?
2. Do tigers live in Niger?
3. What did Ivy decide to do one fine Friday?
4. Why didn't the tiger smile?
5. Where did the tiger dine?
6. Who was smiling at the end of the ride?

Discuss animals with a partner or a group. Talk about your favorite pets and wild animals.

15.9 Listen and Say

There **was** a young **lady** from **Niger,**

Who **smiled** as she **rode** on a **tiger.**

They **returned** from the **ride**

With the **lady inside,**

And the **smile** on the **face** of the **tiger.**

Pair up with a classmate and practice repeating the limerick line by line until you have memorized it. Take turns answering questions about each line and answering with lines from the limerick. Use question words:

Who ... ?

Where ... from?

What did ... ?

Why ... ?

Where ... ?

15.10 Expansion

The names of these wild creatures have the /ay/ sound. Practice saying them.

lion	rhinoceros	magpie
dinosaur	bison	nightingale
viper	porcupine	wildcat
hyena	crocodile	spider

Can you describe them?

In pairs, one person describes a creature from the list above, without naming it, and the other person guesses it.

Check out the meaning of these idioms:

crocodile tears	quiet as a mouse
the lion's share	wise as an owl
cry wolf	blind as a bat
a white elephant	sly as a fox

Make up idioms for your friends.

Example: _____ is as dangerous as a dinosaur.

_____

_____

_____

_____

_____

_____

_____

194

15.11 Read — Letters to Ivy

Dear Ivy,

I saw the story of you and the hungry tiger on a video. I know that he ate you, but don't worry. I have a very strong friend. His name is Hiram Hercules. I told him about you, and he wants to help. Tomorrow Hiram will fly to Niger to get you out of the tiger's stomach.

Hang in there! Everything's going to be all right.

Your friend,

Brian
Cheyenne, Wyoming

Dear Ivy,

I was very sad to hear that it took you three months to recover in the Niger General Hospital. I was very happy to hear that Hiram saved you from that mean, sly tiger. Brian told me that Hiram slugged the tiger and got you out of its stomach. What a fine man he is! And now you're engaged. You certainly do find strange ways to meet guys.

I'm sorry I made that silly bet with you. I shouldn't have dared you to ride on a tiger in Niger. I hope you'll find it in your heart to forgive me. You are a very brave person. I would not have climbed up on its back.

Will you invite me to the wedding?

Sincerely,

Myra

15.12 Write

What do you want to say to Ivy? Write a letter of your own and share it with the class.

Dear Ivy,

15.13 Homonym

What did the wise chef say?

HINT: Thyme is a nice spice.

Notes:

UNIT 16
Ursula

Vowel Focus: /ər/ as in <u>U</u>rsula

She frowned and said, "Now, Mr.!"
Because in sport he kr.
And so, in spite,
That very night,
This Mr. kr. sr.

16.2 Spelling

The sound /ər/ is usually written with the letters *er, ir, or, ur.*

> *er* as in *her, certain, prefer*
> *ir* as in *bird, first, girl*
> *or* as in *word, work, doctor*
> *ur* as in *Thursday, fur, occur*

Examples (listen or read and say):

One syllable: **were** **fir** **word** **fur** **church**
Two syllables: **ker** chief   **thir** sty   **pur** pose   au **thor**
Three syllables: li **ber** ty   de **ter** gent   **per** fec tion
Four syllables: e **mer** gen cy   mo **tor** cy cle

Add some words of your own in the spaces below:

1 Syllable	2 Syllables	3 Syllables	4 Syllables
————	————	————	————
————	————	————	————
————	————	————	————
————	————	————	————
————	————	————	————
————	————	————	————
————	————	————	————

Note: Other spellings are *ear* as in *early, heard, search; our* as in *courage, journey; ar* as in *sugar, coward.*

16.3 Compare Sounds and Words

Compare the vowel sounds in these words.

bird	bored	fur	for
curse	coarse	shirt	short
worm	warm		

Practice reading these sentences aloud with a friend:

1. What's the fur for?
2. Was the bird bored?
3. What did the warm worm ask for?
4. Isn't it coarse to curse?
5. Is my shirt too short?
6. Don't Bert and Ernie work on Sesame Street?
7. Who hurt the turtle?

With a friend, read these words and identify the vowel with the appropriate limerick character.

Example: bird — Ursula

bad	_____	bed	_____	bayed	_____
bead	_____	bid	_____	bus	_____
farm	_____	firm	_____	form	_____
fame	_____	foam	_____	fume	_____
tight	_____	tout	_____	toot	_____
bowl	_____	boil	_____	ball	_____
bull	_____	bell	_____	foot	_____
toy	_____	tea	_____	tie	_____
but	_____	bout	_____	Bert	_____
bat	_____	bit	_____	bought	_____
boot	_____	beaut	_____	Bart	_____

16.4 Vowel Hunt

Which words in these ads use the /ər/ sound?

BERMUDA.
A SHORT TRIP TO
THE PERFECT HOLIDAY.

Jergens
BODY SHAMPOO

IF YOU WANT IT TO BE BETTER,
IT BETTER BE BERTOLLI.
— *Extra Virgin Olive Oil* —

Check your answers with the answers in the back of the book.

16.5 Combine Words to Form Sentences

Read the words in the lists below:

Myrtle	work	Turkey
Ernest	earn	Germany
Gertrude	hurt	Virginia
Kurt	learn	New Jersey
Herbert	flirt	Gibraltar
Shirley	return	Perth

Combine words from each column to form sentences.

Example: Kurt flirted with Shirley in New Jersey.

_____

_____

_____

_____

_____

_____

Some other common /ər/ words are *heard, learned, order, offer, occur, measure, serve, hurt, worry.* Can you make sentences with them?

_____

_____

_____

_____

_____

16.6 Vocabulary

Study the meanings of the following words:

playful: full of fun
mood: feelings at a particular time
sternly: in a strong manner, not gently or with a smile
behave yourself: act in a polite way
get back at someone: to hurt someone who bothered you
besides: in addition, also

Complete the sentences using the words above:

1. He _____ _____ ____ his brother for taking his bicycle without asking.

2. It's a beautiful day, and I'm in a _____.

   _____ Let's have some fun!

   _____, my vacation started today.

3. When you enter a courtroom, you must _____

   _____ .

4. I don't like to listen to him because he speaks so _____ .

Write some sentences with these words:

_____

_____

_____

_____

_____

Look for these words in the story on the next page.

16.7 Read

Ernie

Ernie was in a playful mood and kissed Ursula. Ursula frowned and said sternly, "You'd better behave yourself, Mister." Ernie felt hurt because he was only joking. Besides, he believed that Ursula really liked him. That night, to get back at her, and make her feel worse, Ernie kissed her sister, Gert. How do you think Ursula felt then?

Find 10 different words with the /ər/ sound in the story. List them below:

Check your answers with the answers in the back of the book.

16.8 Speak

Ask and answer these questions with a partner:

1. Why did Ernie kiss Ursula?
2. What did Ursula do?
3. How did Ursula speak?
4. How did Ernie feel?
5. Who was Gert?
6. Discuss flirting. How is it done where you come from?

16.9 Listen and Say

She **frowned** and **said,** "Now, **Mr.**!"

Because in **sport** he **kr.**

And **so,** in **spite,**

That **very night**

This **Mr. kr. sr.**

Pair up with a classmate and practice repeating the limerick line by line until you have memorized it. Take turns answering questions about each line and answering with lines from the limerick. Use question words:

Who … ?

What did … ?

How … ?

16.10 Expansion

The names of many occupations in English are created by adding
-er or *-or* to verbs:

Verb	Noun (occupation)
report	reporter
paint	painter
own	owner
manage	manager
dance	dancer

Add more -er occupations to the list:

_____   _____

_____   _____

_____   _____

_____   _____

Verb	Noun (occupation)
act	actor
inspect	inspector
conduct	conductor
instruct	instructor
counsel	counselor

Add more -or occupations to the list:

_____   _____

_____   _____

_____   _____

_____   _____

16.11 Read — Letters to Ernie and Ursula

Dear Ernie,

I have a question for you. Was it more pleasing to kiss Ursula or her sister? Which one did you prefer? Please tell me why. I'm looking forward to hearing from you.

Yours truly,

Bert
Burlington, Vermont

Dear Ursula,

Do you love Ernie or not? If you love him, don't be too proud. When Ernie kisses you again, you should smile and return his kiss.

Let me know what happens.

Sincerely,

Pearl
Petersburg, Virginia

Dear Ernie,

I heard about last night. I'd like to give you some advice about how a man should treat a woman. Shall we have lunch or dinner soon?

Please call me at 555-6777.

Your friend,

Bertha,
Berlin, New Hampshire

16.12 Write

What do you want to say to Ernie or Ursula? Write a letter of your own and share it with the class.

Dear Ernie [Dear Ursula],

16.13 Homonym

What happened when the cowboy fired his pistol behind his cattle?

HINT: A group of cows is called a *herd*..

Notes:

Review

Without looking back, review Units 11–16 by yourself, with a partner, or with a small group:

- First, tell each character's story.
- Next, try to say the limerick.
- When you have finished, look back at the six units.
- Finally, decidewhich limerick you like best and why. Then discuss your ideas with others.

APPENDIX A
Basic Features of
English Pronunciation

Segmental Sounds

There are 40 different significant sounds in English. They are called **sound segments.** A segment of sound is like the hissing noise of an *s* or the *ah* we make for the doctor when he looks in our mouth.

There are two different kinds of segments: **vowels** and **consonants.** In this book we are focused only on the 16 vowel sounds that a learner of English needs to practice and master. In addition to the 16 vowel sounds that are the focus of this book, there are 24 consonant sounds. For your reference, the consonants are shown on page 217.

Syllables

Syllables are combinations of vowels and consonants. A syllable must have one and only one vowel segment. It does not need a consonant. It can be just a vowel, as in the first part of the name *Ivy:* I*VY. But it can have more than one consonant, as in *Brooke:* BROOKE. In a multisyllable word (at least two syllables), one of the syllables will be louder and longer than the others:

> AD*am
> ex*CEED*ing*ly

Suprasegmental Sounds
Stress

Stress is very important because it helps the listener to understand what you're saying. Native speakers expect the most important words to be emphasized. If you stress the wrong syllable or word, or if you make the syllables and words the same length, it can be very difficult for native speakers to understand you.

Stressed words or syllables are louder, higher, and longer than unstressed ones. Words that are usually stressed are **content words.** They include nouns, verbs, adjectives, and adverbs. Here are some examples of content words:

> *Nouns:* CAN*ner, GRAN*ny, MORN*ing
> *Verbs:* re*MARKED, CAN
> *Adjectives:* CAN*ny
> *Adverbs:* ex*CEED*ing*ly

Words that are usually unstressed are **function words.** They include determiners, prepositions, auxiliary verbs, conjunctions, possessive adjectives, and personal pronouns. The following are examples of function words:

> *Determiners:* a, the
> *Prepositions:* to, in
> *Possessive adjectives: his, her*
> *Auxiliary verbs:* can, will
> *Personal pronouns:* he, she
> *Conjunctions:* and, but

Reduction

In many languages, all the syllables have equal stress. In English, however, if a word has more than one syllable, one syllable is strong (stressed) and the others are weaker (unstressed). The vowel of the unstressed syllable is often reduced to the sound "uh," which is called a *schwa.*

Many prepositions use the schwa — for example:

> of = əv
> for = fər
> to = tə

Function words beginning with *h* are often reduced by dropping the /h/ sound — for example:

> can he? = ken iy?
> didn't he = didn iy?
> kissed her = kist ər

Contractions are examples of reduction in English:

I'm   I'd   I'll   it's   't would   he'd   can't

Linking

In English speech, words in a phrase are said without stops between each word. The words are connected to make a continuous sound. The phrase then sounds like one word because the last letter of one word is joined to the first letter of the next. This often happens with three kinds of phrases:

> *Noun phrase:* a young lady = yəngleydiy
> *Verb phrase:* 't would have been = 'twudəvbin
> *Prepositional phrase:* to his granny = tuwizgraniy

When one vowel is linked to another, the sound of /y/ or /w/ is often used to make the connection:

> the elves = thiyelvz
> so exceedingly neat = soweksiydiŋliy niyt
> be awfully sad = biyɔfulysæd

When a word ends in a consonant, and the next word begins with a vowel, the consonant sound begins the next word:

> and Edward = əndedwərd
> climbed up = klaymdəp
> have ears = heviyrz

When one word ends in a consonant, and the next word begins with the same consonant, it is only pronounced once:

> remarked to = riymarktuw
> and drank = əndræŋk

Intonation

Intonation is the way voices go up (high) and down (low) as we speak. It's like the melody in music.

At the end of sentences that are statements or commands, the voice drops to a low tone:

And kept everything for themselves.

We use intonation that rises to a high tone at the end of a sentence to ask yes–no questions, for requests, and to show doubt or surprise:

He won't up and leave her now, will he?

In a long sentence, the intonation will also be higher on words and syllables that are stressed. Usually the heaviest stress of all (and the highest tone) will be on the last stressed syllable:

And the smile on the face of the tiger.

When a sentence names a list of things, a high pitch is used on all of the things until the last one. Then the voice falls to show the end of the list:

He replied, "At eleven,

At three, five, and seven,

And eight, and a quarter to nine."

Homonyms are words that sound the same, but are spelled differently and have different meanings:

They're glad that **their** friends are all **there.**

English Consonants

SOUND SYMBOL	EXAMPLE	FREQUENT SPELLING
p	pie, apple, lip	p, pp
b	bin, rubber, tub	b, bb
t	tin, butter, but	t, tt
d	din, adder, pad	d, dd
k	kin, kicker, back, cat	k, ck, c
g	gun, bagger, bug	g, gg
f	fall, buffer, rough, phone	f, ff, gh, ph
v	vine, over, love	v
th	thin, both	th
ð	this, other	th
s	sin, kisser, ace	s, ss, c
z	zoo, easy, ways	z, s
sh	she, cash, action	sh, ti
zh	pleasure	s
ch	chin, catch	ch, tch
j	gin, edge	g, dg
m	me, summer, gum	m, mm
n	no, know, in	n, kn
ŋ	sing, singer, bank	ng, n
w	win	w
y	yen	y
l	link, yellow, sell	l
r	ring, carry, car	r, rr
h	hi	h

APPENDIX B
Suggestions for Using the Text
For the Student

This book will help you pronounce the vowel sounds of English. You may already know how to read and write English, and you may have a good knowledge of English grammar and a good vocabulary, but it is essential that you make yourself understood in speaking. Clear pronunciation of vowels is a very important part of speaking. At the same time, developing skill at producing accurate vowel sounds will help you in hearing these sounds and improving your listening comprehension.

Each unit opens with a limerick that highlights a vowel sound. Memorizing and practicing the limericks is important. It will fix the sounds in your mind and help you with the phrasing and melody of English speech. You will recognize which sounds are especially difficult for you. Practice these the most.

You already know that the sounds of English and the spelling of these sounds can be very confusing and frustrating for learners. Each unit begins with work on the various spellings. The exercise gives many examples, but you should add your own examples to the lists. Developing your spelling ability will help with reading and speaking, as well as writing.

Each limerick also has a main character whose name carries the vowel sound of the unit. It is a good idea to use these names when you want to check the pronunciation of a word — for example: "Is this *a* in the word *appendix* the *a* of *Adam*?" (It isn't — it's the *u* of *Gus*.)

The exercises, which cover all skill areas, also use many names and other words that have the vowel sound of the unit. The exercises are designed to make the learning of vowel sounds fun. They will also allow opportunities to use the vowel sound in realistic communicative situations. The answers to the exercises are in the appendix.

One final suggestion: Become familiar with the Unit Outline on page ix. It will help you understand the purpose of the exercises.

For the Teacher

The goal of this text is to help students with the pronunciation of the vowel sounds of North American English. The sounds are presented in the context of limericks. As you well know, it is one thing to produce and recognize sounds in isolation, but the real challenge is in using the sounds in discourse. Using limericks serves to address simultaneously the vowel sounds and the suprasegmental features of stress, reduction, linking, intonation, and the rhythm of English speech. It is important that the students memorize the limericks and repeat them regularly.

The self-explanatory exercises in each unit provide integration of pronunciation with other skill areas. Throughout the exercises, the featured vowel sound occurs again and again as the students speak, listen, read, and write. The exercises also serve to provide practice of the vowel sound in communicative situations, such as paired conversations, guessing games, role plays, and reading and writing letters. At the same time, they are designed to be entertaining and to create an atmosphere of fun in the classroom.

Here are some suggestions for enhancing the text:

- *Personalize* the material:
  - Use the sounds in the students' own names, addresses, native cities, and countries.
- *Capitalize* on students' talents:
  - Ask the students to illustrate incidents in the limerick, new vocabulary, humorous sentences, etc.
  - Sing songs that emphasize the targeted sound, such as "Oh, Susannah!"
- *Dramatize* the limericks.
- *Elasticize* the material to include words that students contribute from their real-life experiences.
- *Organize* the classroom work for the students, following the sequence in the units. Provide model pronunciation, but let the students follow directions, ask, read, write, practice, and be creative with the material. The goal is improved pronunciation, so let the students do the talking.

APPENDIX C
Answers to Exercises

UNIT 1 **Adam**

1.3 Compare Sounds and Words

/æ/	/a/	/ə/
mad		mud
slap	slop	
battle	bottle	
spatter	spotter	sputter
stack	stock	stuck
Jan	John	
knack	knock	
sandy		Sunday
sax	socks	sucks
tap	top	
shack	shock	shuck
bat		but
black	block	
lag	log	lug

1.4 Vowel Hunt
#1 actress, Anjelica, Addams Family Values
#2 antiques, January, Saturday, and
#3 annual, Scandinavian
#4 actor, Anthony, Angeles, National
#5 Back, land, natural

1.6 Vocabulary
1. canner, exceedingly, canny
2. Preservation
3. chat
4. remarked, granny

1.7 Read   *17 different /æ/ sounds:* Adam, apples, apricots, carrots, asparagus, salmon, canner, Saturday, January, chatting, grandmother, has, asks, one can, to can, granny, laughs
Note: *can* in *he can put* is not stressed, and the vowel becomes /ə/.

1.9 Listen and Say

Word	*Number*	*Stressed Syllable*
canner	2	1st
exceedingly	4	2nd
canny	2	1st
morning	2	1st
remarked	2	2nd
granny	2	1st
anything	3	1st

1.10 Expansion
1. Granny cans (verb)   2. a can of apples (noun)
3. Granny can make (modal auxiliary verb)

1.13 Homonym   A 14-carat carrot

UNIT 2 *Edna and Edward*
2.3 Compare Sounds and Words

1. mat	4. sad	7. Annie	10. ten
2. left	5. said	8. sand	11. laughed
3. pen	6. head	9. shell	12. met

2.4 Vowel Hunt
#1 Lexus, relentless, perfection   #2 friends, Fred, lessons, special
#3 Guess, collection

2.6 Vocabulary
memorable, treasure, shelf, elves, merry, pleasure, selfish

2.7 Read
20 words: Edna, Edward, merry, clever, elves, adventure, memorable, Wednesday, entered, many, shelves, shelf, pleasure, objects, incredible, treasure, guess, kept, everything, themselves

2.9 Listen and Say

Word	Number	Stressed Syllable
Edna	2	1st
Edward	2	1st
elves	1	1st
shelves	1	1st
treasure	2	1st
pleasure	2	1st
everything	3	1st

2.10 Expansion
wives, lives, leaves, calves, thieves, scarves, knives, loaves
1. scarves   2. lives   3. calves   4. leaves   5. thieves   6. wives
7. knives   8. loaves

2.13 Homonym
He sent her a scent.

UNIT 3 *Amy*
3.3 Compare Sounds and Words
raid/red, braid/bread, mate/met, fade/fed, saint/cent, whale/well, waste/west, wait/wet, late/let, tailor/teller

3.4 Vowel Hunt
#1 Macy's   #3 paper, everyday_____#5 Grape
#2 sale, savings   #4 say, Delaney

3.6 Vocabulary
1. shape, undone, sunbathing   2. wrinkled   3. famous, graceful   4. "What a shame!"

3.7 Read
16 words: Amy, tasty, grape, famous, graceful, shape, day, vacation, lazy, place, stayed, eight, sunbathing, changed, raisin, shame

---

UNIT 3 *Amy (continued)*
3.9 Listen and Say

Word	*Number*	*Stressed Syllable*
Amy	2	1st
graceful	2	1st
shape	1	1st
bathed	1	1st
undone	2	2nd
raisin	2	1st
shame	1	1st

3.10 Expansion *undone:* 1. new building … not finished 2. her bow … unfastened 3. Amy's shape … ruined

3.13 Homonym Eight ate.

UNIT 4 **Rita**

4.4 Vowel Hunt
#1 Citibank, Citi, sleeps
#2 antiques
#3 beef, real, people
#4 Easter, Tiffany's please

4.6 Vocabulary
1. Crete … neat
2. make sure … soil
3. seem
4. extremely

4.7 Read *12 words:* Rita, neat, clean, lady, Greek, Crete, she, extremely, clean, feet, keep, weird

4.9 Listen and Say

Word	*Number*	*Stressed Syllable*
lady	2	1st
Crete	1	1st
exceedingly	4	2nd
neat	1	1st
soiling	2	1st

4.13 Homonym To peek at the peak.

UNIT 5 **Billy**

5.3 Compare Sounds and Words
1. mitt 3. ten 5. knit 7. pet 9. seed
2. meat 4. tin 6. teen 8. neat 10. pit

5.4 Vowel Hunt
#1 Clint, Bridges
#2 Singapore, Pacific
#3 Finnair, individual

5.6 Vocabulary
1. carrier pigeon
2. deliver
3. Chilean … smitten

UNIT 5 **Billy** *(continued)*

5.7 Read *21 words:* pigeon, Billy, Finland, His, bring, quickly, windy, wintry, delivers, Chile, pretty, Chilean, is, Linda, in, minute, smitten, big, it, impossible, him

5.10 Crossword

Across	3. wasn't it		7. didn't she		11. aren't I
	6. wouldn't they		9. won't they		14. should we
					15. is he

Down	1. can't I		5. isn't she		11. am I
	2. do you		8. have we		12. is it
	3. shouldn't it		10. will I		13. do I

5.13 Homonym Jim's gyms.

UNIT 6 **Gus**

6.3 Compare Sounds and Words

1. bug		4. nut		7. knit	
2. knot		5. net		8. beg	
3. big		6. tech		9. tick, tock	10. bog

6.4 Vowel Hunt

#1 Cuts
#2 Chanel
#3 Sotheby's, Avenue
#4 Phantom of the Opera, Majestic

6.6 Vocabulary

1. replied		4. dine
2. glutton		5. reply
3. Rhine		

6.7 Read *Stressed (6 words):* Gus, hundred, twenty-one, glutton, much, hungry__*Unstressed (7 words):* was, a, from, the, often, replied, different *Both stressed and stressed:* glutton

6.9 Listen and Say

Word	Number	Stressed Syllable
glutton	2	1st
replied	2	2nd
eleven	3	2nd
seven	2	1st
quarter	2	1st

Words in the limerick with unstressed /ə/:

glutton	Was	eleven	the
from	what	seven	replied

6.13 Homonym One won.

7.3 Compare Sounds and Words

1. pot	4. sax	7. knock
2. neck	5. tack	8. socks
3. six	6. pat	9. rock 10. wreck

7.4 Vowel Hunt

#1 Document, Xerox

#2 operation, drop

#3 astonishing, Tom, Ron, Apollo, Garner

7.6 Vocabulary

1. ostrich	4. spread
2. waste	5. energy
3. imitate	6. Don't bother

7.7 Read *10 words:* Oscar, ostrich, wanted, watched, got, off, father, sorry, stop, impossible

7.9 Listen and Say /a/ *words in the limerick:*

Oscar	father	bother
ostrich	Oscar	honestly

7.13 Homonym The heart of the hart.

8.4 Vowel Hunt

#1 warm, Norman, your	#4 Nordstrom, mall, short
#2 North, shore, port	#5 Oral, fluoride, formulate
#3 water, forty	

8.5 Combine Words to Form Sentences *Simple past of irregular verbs:*

bring/brought	buy/bought	catch/caught	
fight/fought	think/thought	teach/taught	seek/sought

8.6 Vocabulary

1. although	3. fall	5. cough
2. Springs	4. unfortunately	6. fall

8.7 Read *10 different words:* Paul, water, all, long, fall, walking, caught, coughing, falling, although

8.10 1. E. fall for   2. H. fell short   3. B. fall back on   4. J. falls under
5. F. falling off   6. A. fall back   7. D. fell flat   8. G. falling out
9. C. falling behind   10. I. fallen through

8.13 Homonym Its paws pause.

UNIT 9 *Joe*
9.4 Vowel Hunt
#1 tr<u>o</u>ve, G<u>o</u>bi   #3 Sm<u>o</u>key J<u>oe</u>'s
#2 Pian<u>o</u>, L<u>oe</u>ws, sh<u>ow</u>place   #4 t<u>o</u>tal, neg<u>o</u>tiator

9.6 Vocabulary
1. prefers   2. rather
3. emotional, hold on to   4. suppose, heartbroken, bald

9.7 Read   *13 different words:* supp<u>o</u>se, J<u>oe</u>, j<u>o</u>king, t<u>oe</u>s, n<u>o</u>se, d<u>o</u>n't, em<u>o</u>tional, h<u>o</u>lding, heartbr<u>o</u>ken, g<u>oe</u>s, h<u>o</u>pes, <u>o</u>lder, w<u>o</u>n't

9.10 Expansion   1. like very   2. to prefer   3. instead of

9.13 Homonym   He was thrown off the throne.

UNIT 10 *Roy*
10.3 Compare Sounds and Words   soy, fail, see, toil, aisle, sigh, foil, eel, tale

10.4 Vowel Hunt
#1 ch<u>oi</u>ce   #3 v<u>oy</u>ages   #5 M<u>oy</u>ers
#2 T<u>oy</u>ota   #4 R<u>oy</u>al

10.6 Vocabulary
1. avoid   3. boisterous   5. recognize
2. roots   4. joy, rejoiced

10.7 Read   *8 different words:* R<u>oy</u>, B<u>oi</u>se, n<u>oi</u>sy, v<u>oi</u>ce, n<u>oi</u>se, av<u>oi</u>ded, rej<u>oi</u>ced, J<u>oi</u>se

10.13 Homonym   They roil the royal family.

UNIT 11 *Brooke*
11.4 Vowel Hunt
#1 G<u>oo</u>dy   #2 b<u>oo</u>k   #3 w<u>oo</u>l   #4 Br<u>oo</u>ks

11.6 Vocabulary
1. furious   3. habit   5. antics
2. frantic   4. curious

11.7 Read   *10 different words:* Br<u>oo</u>ke, Ast<u>u</u>rias, w<u>oo</u>l, c<u>u</u>shions, p<u>u</u>dding, c<u>oo</u>kies, g<u>oo</u>d, f<u>u</u>rious, sh<u>ou</u>ldn't, c<u>ou</u>ldn't

11.13 Homonym   Mr. Wood would.

UNIT 12 **Louis**

12.3 Compare Sounds and Words
1. look   3. so   5. blood   7. cook
2. no   4. put   6. sew

12.4 Vowel Hunt
#1 movie, fleur, cuckoo   #3 hoop, two
#2 Bloomingdale's, shoes   #4 Mitsubishi

12.6 Vocabulary
1. nutritious   2. to-do   3. includes, stew   4. wave, about

12.7 Read *12 different words:* cool, June, Louis, stew, nutritious, foods, truly, to-do, cool, choose, too, foolish

12.13 Homonym It flew into a flue.

UNIT 13 **Ulysses**

13.3 Compare Sounds and Words
1. Hugh   3. hues   5. whose and who   7. mute
2. fuel   4. mood   6. a fool   8. cute

13.4 Vowel Hunt
#1 Beauty, musical   #2 Computer   #3 mutual

13.6 Vocabulary
1. contribute   3. exceptions   5. ukelele
2. amusing   4. reputation, stubborn

13.7 Read *13 different words:* Dukedom, Eureka, mule, Ulysses, reputation, refused, usual, duke, museum, music, usually, ukelele, amused

13.13 Homonym Stop it! You aren't a ewe, are you?

UNIT 14 **Ms. Brown**

14.3 Compare Sounds and Words *words with the /aw/ sound:* gown, doubt, down, couch, chowder, crowd, flower, pow-wow, powder, proud, know-how, eyebrow, rout, round

14.4 Vowel Hunt
#1 how, without   #2 mouse, house   #3 outer, outstanding

14.6 Vocabulary 1. mean   2. astounded   3. bounce   4. curious

14.7 Read *10 different words:* Howard, astounded, Ms. Brown, house, round, how, pounds, ounces, down, bounce

UNIT 14 **Ms. Brown** *(continued)*
14.10 Abbreviations
1. ave.   3. NBC   5. OPEC   7. TWA   9. Jr.
2. U.N.   4. dept.   6. M.A.   8. St.

14.13 Homonym   A flour flower.

UNIT 15 **Ivy**
15.4 Vowel Hunt
#1 timing, delightful, Times, Simon, Ives   #2 Dime
#3 styles, times

15.6 Vocabulary
1. delighted, frowned   3. Niger, spend, isolated   2. wild, jungle

15.7 Read   *22 different words:* Ivy, life, Niger, wild, fine, Friday, July, decided, ride, tiger, smiled, delight, while, delighted, besides, quite, isolated, dined, inside, smiling, time, smile

15.13 Homonym   It's time for the thyme.

UNIT 16 **Ursula**
16.3 Compare Words and Sounds

bad — Adam	bed — Edna	bayed — Amy
bead — Rita	bid — Billy	bus — Gus
farm — Oscar	firm — Ursula	form — Paul
fame — Amy	foam — Joe	fume — Ulysses
tight — Ivy	tout — Mr. Brown	toot — Louis
bowl — Joe	boil — Roy	ball — Paul
bull — Brooke	bell — Edna	foot — Brooke
toy — Roy	tea — Rita	tie — Ivy
but — Gus	bout — Mr. Brown	Bert — Ursula
bat — Adam	bit — Billy	bought — Paul
boot — Louis	beaut — Ulysses	Bart — Oscar

16.4 Vowel Hunt
#1 Bermuda, perfect   #2 Jergens   #3 better, Bertolli, virgin

16.6 Vocabulary
1. got back at   3. behave yourself
2. playful, mood, Besides   4. sternly

16.7 Read   *10 different words:* Ernie, Ursula, sternly, better, mister, hurt, her, worse, sister, Gert

16.13 Homonym   The herd heard.

Also Available
from Pro Lingua Associates

Pronunciation Card Games by Linnea Henry.

Using photocopyable cards from the book, the 16 games help students (1) to improve their production and discrimination of difficult vowel and consonant sounds (segmentals) and (2) to distinguish and produce major and minor stress, reduction, and emphatic stress (suprasegmental aspects of pronunciation). Specific games are recommended for speakers of 20 major languages; *photocopyable.*

Conversation Inspirations: Over 2000 Conversation Topics by Nancy Zelman.

A teacher resource with 8 different conversation class activities: talks, interviews, discussions, and role plays, chain stories and other group activities. Procedures for each are clearly laid out. These include the use of topic cards, monitoring, correction techniques, and a variety of game rituals that make the conversation class effective and enjoyable. Inexpensive, quick, and easy to use; *photocopyable.*

Two student texts by David Kehe and Peggy Dustin Kehe.

Conversation Strategies: Pair and Group Activities for Developing Communicative Competence *and* **Discussion Strategies:** Beyond Everyday Conversation

These are integrated skills texts. The first, for intermediate level students, has 24 activities giving practice with the words, phrases, and conventions used to participate in and maintain some effective control of conversations. The second book, for high-intermediate to advanced students, has 38 activities with clear, step-by-step, focused practice of 13 discussion skills needed at high academic and business levels: using rejoinders, asking follow-up questions, seeking/giving clarification, using comprehension checks, soliciting and using details, interrupting, expressing opinions, volunteering answers, referring to information and opinion sources, helping discussion leaders, and leading a discussion. Students work in real discussion formats – pairs, triads, small groups, and whole class. The discussion topics are drawn from real, amusing, high interest articles; no depth of background knowledge is needed.

All of the above resources for developing pronunciation and conversation skills are available from **Pro Lingua Associates** *.com*

PO Box 1348, Brattleboro, Vermont 05302 USA • 800 366 4775